8/02

an emotional memoir of martha quinn

an emotional memoir of martha quinn

by alan licht

drag city incorporated / chicago

Alan Licht by "Klaus" (2001)

Introduction

If you're reading this book to find out what MTV VJ Martha Quinn was really like, I've got some tough news for you. I've never met Martha Quinn. The title is a reference to a book by Fielding Dawson called *An Emotional Memoir of Franz Kline*. Martha was the network's girl next door type*—a cutie who liked Paul McCartney very much (as do I), and I think she dated Billy Idol for a spell. To my knowledge, her story has never been told; the fact that, despite the title, I will not be telling it is the first and possibly last disappointment you will find herein.

What follows is a highly subjective survey of the last two decades as seen through my prism as a music performer, listener, scenester, and occasionally, writer. It traces the changes in the New York and national underground music scenes, paralleling my personal journey through adolescence to adulthood. To be sure, the role this stuff played in my life, the culture in general, and the music industry has gone through a tremendous evolution. For me, some of these "changes" are as much a progression from fantasy to reality as anything. What might come off as judgmental in these pages is not intended that way. I'm simply recording my adult experiences vs. my teenage expectations of playing music in the real world. To be sure, the world has changed a lot since the early Eighties, as has my little corner of it; I've tried to sort out which is which for you (and myself) the best I can.

Pete Townshend once said that he could talk for hours about Meher Baba (his guru), or politics, or what have you, but he saw it all "through two slits marked rock and roll." You should keep this in mind as you read on, especially in the sections where I stray from mere music writing into (ahem) larger issues. This ain't no history book or political tract, it's a remembrance of things past by one of what Kim Wilde used to call "The Kids in America."

Alan Licht
New York, August 2001

---

*Nina Blackwood was the faux-hipster siren, Mark Goodman was the nice Jewish boy turned metalhead, J.J. Jackson was the Black Guy, and Alan Hunter was the Guy With the Same First Name as Me.

"Would someone with a hard face protect me
from those sickly and sugared old tunes?"

Dennis Potter

"That techno-rock you guys listen to is gutless!"

Randy (Nicholas Cage), a "punk," to Julie (Deborah Freeman),
a "valley girl," in the film **Valley Girl**, 1983.

DANCE HALL DAYS, 1998

Sitting in a pizzeria in Hoboken one day in March, The Thompson Twins' "Hold Me Now" comes on the radio. I haven't heard it in fourteen years or so, but, like seeing an old photograph or memento, the details start to fill in moment by moment. As it plays on I start to remember every word, every nuance—the bridge, the big piano flourish in the third verse, then those falsetto backing vocals in the last verse that add "cold and tired" to "my heart." The guy's voice seems so blunt and dull, but god, it's a good song. I tried to imagine myself as a producer, suggesting the falsetto stuff or the piano fill, but

I couldn't do it. Plus, I thought it was Modern English when the song came on. I don't remember every frame of a movie I saw fifteen years ago (although I remembered more of *Splash* than I would have thought when I saw it again on cable), why do I remember so much of "Hold Me Now"? You can forget about a song, but never really forget it. Obviously I heard it many times back in the day. I've also noticed when on tour with various bands that watching their sets night after night I begin to like the songs I didn't like or care about at first. In fourth grade, I used to hear "The Closer I Get To You" by Roberta Flack and Donny Hathaway on the radio ten times a day, every day, for a month: I couldn't stand it. But by the end of the month, I actually liked the song; I still like it.

Shopping in the supermarket a couple of weeks later, I notice that the muzak version of "I Melt With You" by Modern English is on. I remember seeing this video many times, not quite buying the song's likability or optimism or the singer's faux-punk image (sleeveless black T-shirt and cap). However, his skinniness gave me comfort as a terminally scrawny adolescent (and now adult), as did Mick Jones's (who I used to resemble with my parentally enforced short hair), Iggy's on the *Raw Power* cover, and Mick Jagger's. It's a memorable song, though. I've always liked the hummed repetition of the guitar solo when everything else drops out, followed by the drum fill that kicks the song into its final gear. Thinking about it now, it's kind of a peppier "Heroes," borrowing the Robert Fripp guitar lead and everything. Watered down Bowie—who was pretty watered down to begin with.

I watch Eddie Money do "Two Tickets to Paradise" on the *Rosie O'Donnell Show* about a month after the Thompson Twins incident. He looks ghoulish and lounge-singer-y, lots of "How ya doin' out there?" between lines of the song. But when he sat down with Rosie he looked normal again. When he went back onstage to sing again, he looked weird. I remember seeing him on *Kids Are People Too*, saying how his real name was Eddie Mahoney, how he became a cop to dodge the draft, and how one side of his mouth was paralyzed. I was not an Eddie Money fan, I can't believe I've retained this knowledge to this day. Driving up to the Nihilist Spasm Band's No Music Festival in London, Ontario, I hear two E.M. songs on the radio. How curious. I also hear "Voices Carry" by 'Til Tuesday, a song I liked when it came out, but unlike "Hold Me Now," I don't remember anything except the chorus. Originally I thought she was singing "You're So Scary," but upon learning the name of the song, I realized my mistake.

Not long after these incidents, Falco died in a car accident. His big hit was "Der Kommissar," sung in his native German. I vividly remember the cheesy video for the song, where he lip-synched in mirror shades, a white T-shirt, and jeans against a bad rear projection of Berlin-at-night-by-car footage. I liked the vocal in the original German, although the American remake by After the Fire had better production—less Eurodisco-y, with some nice acoustic guitar strumming during one break. Nena's "99 Luftballoons" sounded cool in German, but then the English version (again by Nena) came out and revealed the lyrics to be totally weak anti-nuke/war junk. You know, the red balloons are mistaken for missiles and WWIII starts.

Suddenly, for the first time in close to a decade, the Eighties were back in my life. Like Philip K. Dick flashing on ancient Rome superimposed on 1974 California by seeing a fish-shaped piece of jewelry (an ancient Christian symbol) worn by his pharmacist's delivery girl, I felt the presence of the Eighties, still a reality underneath the surface of the late Nineties.

Somehow remembering every nuance of a "bad" new wave hit from the early Eighties that I never felt much connection to gives me more pleasure than remembering every moment of, I don't know, a favorite punk single I haven't listened to in a while. I know all of them from watching hours and hours of MTV in my early teens, which coincided with its emergence on cable in August of 1981, praying for "Radio Clash" or "Rock the Casbah" to come on (or "Public Image," which the trés hip Nina Blackwood would play every now and then). Everybody watched MTV in school, and everybody knew all the songs they played incessantly, one of the few bonding experiences I could stomach back then. The irony is that I like stuff like the Thompson Twins better now when I hear it than I do "Radio Clash" or "Rock the Casbah." The Clash's "alternative" stance reflected my own emerging identity back then, but now as a lifetime member of the non-mainstream community, it seems that the garbage I endured waiting for my idols to come on MTV has left a bigger impact on my psyche than I would have guessed. I squeezed a lot of listenability out of the MTV playlist, despite the fact that I never bought any records based on MTV—in fact, I was buying stuff like X, Richard Hell, MC5, the Stooges, Beefheart, PiL, Dream Syndicate, the Velvet Underground, the Sex Pistols, the Ramones, the New York Dolls, Gang of Four, and Joy Division.

Trying to listen to "new wave" artists like Elvis Costello, the Police, R.E.M., Graham Parker, U2, as "punk" was hopeless, although for some reason I tried anyway. I was looking for excitement and edginess, and that's pretty much the best that broadcast media could come up with. The Pretenders mixed punk with jangly guitar pop in a way I still find inspiring, at least when I hear their old records (my guitar solo on Run On's "Days Away" is a tribute to the one on "Private Life"). I heard an Elvis Costello rock block—"Pump It Up," "Radio Radio," "(What's So Funny 'Bout) Peace, Love and Understanding?"—recently, and it sounded great, better than it ever did when I was trying to hear it as punk. Just good rock. And, like the Police or Joe Jackson, another good compromise back in the day. Kinda punk, kinda Sixties-ish, kinda reggae—in other words, something with quality that OTHER PEOPLE KNEW ABOUT TOO in high school.

I knew Billy Idol had been in a punk band (Generation X) because when I was 10 my cousin had given me the book *1988*, by Caroline Coon, all about the '77 British punk scene. The book scared the shit out of me at first—I literally could not look at one photo of Joey Ramone—but eventually I got familiar with all the different bands in it, and eventually, interested in hearing them (starting with the Clash, who showed up on the radio with "London Calling" a year or two later). So, right, Billy Idol—I followed his MTV career with interest. "Rebel Yell" and "White Wedding" are decent songs, with faint traces of punk in them, and of course Billy's Alan Vega-derived (as I learned later) sneers and screams. Once I heard Suicide, I didn't need no Billy Idol—but that was four years later, as a freshman in college. "Eyes Without A Face" heard in the Nineties sorta sounded like My Bloody Valentine. I knew Joan Jett from the *1988* book too—there's a picture of her with a ball and chain that says SEX PISTOLS on it. Her records were pretty powerful, probably better than the Runaways (who I've never heard). "Bad Reputation" could be the Ramones, I really dug her power chord remake of Sly Stone's "Everyday People," too. This stuff was on MTV all the time back then, especially "Crimson and Clover" (Billy Idol covered Tommy Shondell too—"Mony Mony") and "I Love Rock and Roll." There was also Pete Shelley of the Buzzcocks with "Homosapien," which seemed kinda punk but was really quite new wave in retrospect. Lords of the New Church (Stiv Bators from the Dead Boys and Brian James from the Damned) were more on a goth tip like Siouxsie & the Banshees ("Spellbound" is a great song that got a fair amount of MTV play back then), or Sisters of Mercy, or the Damned (neither of whom made it onto MTV too much, although the Damned's Captain Sensible had a novelty song, "Wot," that was on MTV pretty frequently, consisting of little besides "they said 'Captain'/I said 'Wot'"). Kevin Rowland, who cut a scorching '77 single with the Killjoys, donned some overalls, corralled a couple of violinists, formed Dexy's Midnight Runners, and scored a hit with "Come On Eileen," a song which I still find irritating as hell. There was also Bow Wow Wow, managed by Malcolm McLaren, whose tribal new wave holds up pretty well (at least "C30 C60 C90 Go" does); "I Want Candy" was another video I used to look for. I haven't heard McLaren's own stab at hip-hop, "Buffalo Gals," in ages, but most likely it sux. In essence, the stars of '77 punk (the big party I'd missed) weren't faring much better musically than the stars of Sixties classic rock were in the Eighties, at least compared to past glories. As one book title put it, it was like punk never happened. No wonder us "slackers" were so dang cynical!

MY PARENTS WENT TO WOODSTOCK, AND ALL I GOT WAS THIS LOUSY CULTURE CLUB ALBUM

I resented a lot of MTV music at the time because it paled next to the Sixties classics I would hear on WPLJ or WNEW. Listening to it now I realize it's totally rooted in that music, just disguised under tragically misguided production values. The Jesus and Mary Chain (a real sign of life for me back in '85) buried good Sixties-style pop songs under feedback and noise (taking the Ramones formula to its avant apex). Human League, Soft Cell, et al. buried them under synths and drum machines. Yuppies and baby boomers had all the media attention back then, how they used to be free-spirited hippies and now were money-grubbing neo-conservatives. Not too inspiring. The recording industry was like that too—they didn't really know how to deal with rock in the Sixties, but in the Seventies it became big business. Don Henley's "Boys of Summer" captured it perfectly—a Sixties kid turned Seventies star doing a total Eighties hit trip, talking about seeing "a Deadhead sticker on a Cadillac." It always belonged in a time capsule. There was a tremendous emphasis on nostalgia for the era of their youth—*The Big Chill* really hit a nerve. I remember when people like Sting and Bono started to wear their hair long again, and Prince did *Around the World in a Day*—this kind of, like, totally ersatz return to the garden, to paraphrase Joni Mitchell. Everyone wanted the Sixties party to start up again, but the US Festival, Farm Aid, and Live Aid sure weren't Woodstock, and Springsteen and Mellencamp sure weren't Dylan and Fogerty, and Stevie Ray Vaughan sure wasn't Eric Clapton or Jimi Hendrix, and U2 sure wasn't the Beatles, and Tom Petty & the Heartbreakers sure weren't the Byrds, and Prince wasn't Sly Stone (or was he?). And the stars of the Sixties made total shit music in the Eighties—Clapton,

Steve Winwood, McCartney, Jagger, CSNY, the Who, the Starship, Iggy, Lou Reed. In the face of this, I looked to the SST bands for a real take on the true legacy of the Sixties, another big party I'd missed. For these bands rock was still a way of life, not a lifestyle accessory: the Meat Puppets' acid-soaked take on Neil Young's career pattern, Hüsker Dü careening through "Eight Miles High," Black Flag or the Minutemen as a people's band à la the MC5 (Rollins growing his hair long was actually a turning point in the underground as Flag's Sabbath influence became more pronounced sonically)—that was where the boomers should have been looking for their lost youth. Sure, Huey Lewis was from San Francisco, and there was a version of "I Want a New Drug" with extended guitar solos on it that was pretty good as I recall—Chris Hayes, one of the lead guitarists, was a jazzbo turned rocker for the $$$ (just like one of my heroes, Elliot Easton of the Cars, or Andy Summers of the Police) and he was also the brother of Bonnie Hayes, a Slash recording artist who did "Girls Like Me," best remembered as the theme song to the classic teen film *Valley Girl*, but you didn't really need to know that, did you?—but they weren't the inheritors of Quicksilver and the Airplane; Sonic Youth was (among other things). The hardcore kids of the Eighties—the ones in the mosh pits at matinee shows, corresponding with *Maximum Rock and Roll*, what have you—were, despite punk's avowed anti-hippie stance, the hippies of the Eighties, and now poised to become the yuppies of the new millennium as they assume their positions at every dot-com under the sun (if a 20-year-old college dropout doesn't get there first). For people of my generation, born in the Sixties, the decade loomed throughout adolescence like some departed relative we were too young to know but who was still discussed endlessly. Where was I when JFK was shot? Sorry, not born yet—although I *was* born mere hours after

Robert Kennedy was shot (my mother even mistook the labor pains for an upset stomach from the news). The children of the hippies were really their cultural younger siblings.

———————

Finding a good song underneath the slick, big-entertainment value system of pop radio—whether it was Madonna's hits, or "Time After Time" by Cyndi Lauper, or Michael Jackson, or "Africa" by Toto, or "Inside Out" by Phil Collins—was fun. I wonder if it would still be fun now. I'm no rock critic, I don't feel compelled to monitor what people are listening to; I don't have a car, so I don't hear much radio, and I haven't watched MTV since the early Nineties. And I have a lot more options now for music and everything else. As an adolescent, you live where your parents want to live, have to go to school, you make friends based more or less on who's in the school. You don't necessarily know all the possibilities that are out there in the world. To an extent, you're dependent on broadcast media to learn about what's out there when you're 13 or 14 years old. In a way commercial radio and MTV were the perfect soundtrack for the jail sentence of suburban adolescence. Making the best of this crap was a lot like making the best out of a suburban junior high school crowded with the sons and daughters of Republican doctors and lawyers in an Old Money town where certain sections weren't shown by realtors to Jewish families (like mine, although there was a large Jewish population there). But I was also reading *The Village Voice* at that age, so I had some sense of life beyond the mall. As an adult, I live where I want to live, work where I want to work, I have friends all over the world. There's no reason for me to try and squeeze some listenability out of whatever's on the radio or watch MTV—there are a million alternatives available to me, especially in NYC. It took me years to find out that the instrumental sections I liked in "Light My Fire," "In Memory of Elizabeth Reed," or "Southern Man" were inspired by John Coltrane. Because of my dedication to music, I found out eventually—most people probably don't. But that's fine, and I don't like those songs any less just because I discovered their jazz roots.

Also, this broadcast media made the fantasy of being a rock star possible. Aside from the kids in my bands or a couple of other friends at school, the only people I "knew" who played guitar were on records or TV—if that was the only competition, and if I could play what they were playing (and I could), it was only logical that I would be following in their footsteps. It didn't seem like such a long distance between being the hot guitarist in school and being on the cover of *Guitar Player*. Now everytime I walk out of my apartment, I see ten guys with gig bags strapped across their shoulders. Who knew that everybody else wants to be a rock star too? Growing up, I was practically the only one.

———

As the months passed, the hits just kept on coming:

Quarterflash, "Harden My Heart"
Heard it on the office manager's radio at work today for the first time in ages, liked it okay when it came out. Didn't remember the harmony vocal on the chorus. The "darling, in my wildest dreams" part has a nice melody, then the singer blows it with too many "know—oo-oh-whoah"s (not to mention "new—oo-hoo-oo-oo-woo-ooh"s). The chorus and guitar response are generic, but "I'm gonna turn and

le—heave you-hoo here" has another nice melody, which reverses the "darling" one, so I'm hooked. Tasty sax and guitar solos, too. Overall I don't like this record—the singer's annoying, the band is lame. But there's stuff in it I like.

Dire Straits, "Money for Nothing"

CBGB's, April '98, Royal Trux is playing. CB's is now just another rock bar. This place used to stand for something, now it could be just any other joint on Bleecker Street. The Trux close their set with a cover of Dire Strait's 1983 classic "Money For Nothing," the first hit song to reference the MTV phenomenon. Neil's voice sounds uncannily like Mark Knopfler's. If they'd played it ten years ago, it would have been an obvious punk rock joke, like the woeful hardcore band 7 Seconds covering "99 Luftballoons." Now it's striking how similar it is to their own songs. When Neil Hagerty sings, "We got to move these refrigerators/we got to move these color TVs," he could almost be singing about RTX as a touring band, loading their own gear in and out of clubs night after night, year after year. Knopfler sang the song as a self-deprecating joke, as the one making money for nothing "on the MTV."

In fact that was when I gave up on Dire Straits. I liked "Sultans of Swing" (which I originally took to be a new Clapton single when it first came out) and *Making Movies*. Even had a social studies teacher in seventh grade who liked 'em (and who also, we were convinced, prayed to the sun). She was also partial to Lowell George and some of my very Jim Morrison–damaged poetry. Anyway, by the time "Money for Nothing" came out, they were totally keyboard-dominated, Eighties mersh style. Ten years later I watched some of a Dire Straits concert on TV in Switzerland, on tour with Love Child. They were so lifeless onstage that every little gesture became totally dramatic, like they were giving little clues about themselves to the audience. Like when the Empire State Building's lights go on in Warhol's *Empire* after an hour. I remember thinking about the bass player, how anyone could play bass in this band, he just got lucky when he hitched his star to Knopfler's wagon. (Okay, I think it was his brother.)

The Fixx, "One Thing Leads to Another"

I don't think I liked this song much when it came out, but I like it a lot now. I remember liking their other hit, "Red Skies," (another anti-nuke/war song I think) better, but basically they're fairly nondescript. "One Thing" is a pretty good Roxy Music/Talking Heads circa *Remain in Light* combo—I like the part where the drums drop out and the backup vocals take up the rhythm.

Billy Joel, "Allentown"

I totally forgot about this song until I saw the video again at my parents' house, on VH1's Pop Up Video show. The video is ludicrous (think Thomas Hart Benton meets Supertramp's "It's Raining Again" video), lots of dancers with a kind of Hallmark version of *The Deer Hunter* "plot." I was shocked to find myself liking the song a lot—I've always hated Joel, although I liked "Big Shot" when it came out. In fact, I used to insist on turning the volume up in the car radio on family trips to Boston to visit my grandparents in 1978 whenever "Big Shot" or "Who Are You?" came on—by the end of the ride it was deafening! I remember one WFMU fundraising drive where the Hound threatened to play Billy Joel unless people called in with pledges. For a long time it was impossible to enter a restaurant in New York where they played the radio without hearing a Billy Joel song sometime during the course of the meal. Anyway, "Allentown" was stuck in my head for the rest of the day so forcefully that I think it actually woke me up the next morning.

Phil Collins & Philip Bailey, "Easy Lover"

This is a great song; I only remembered the chorus until I heard it on the radio recently. Collins is an odd figure; a journeyman prog-rocker (Genesis, Brand X, even Eno's *Taking Tiger Mountain by Strategy*) turned noxious, sappy hit-maker. I remember seeing some footage of one of his concerts on TV where he just ran back and forth on the huge stage singing his songs. Is that entertainment?

Rod Stewart, "Young Turks"

Along with "Bette Davis Eyes," this is a quintessential seventh grade song for me—or was it eighth grade? Pretty cool that Rod seems to champion teenage pregnancy here ("Don't let 'em put you down, don't let 'em push you around/Don't ever let them change your point of view"), and my friend Aaron has correctly posited this as one of the great rock/disco hits (certainly better than Stewart's earlier, icky "If You Think I'm Sexy," and right up there with Kiss's "I Was Made for Loving You," the Stones' "Miss You," Nick Lowe's original (45) version of "Cruel to Be Kind," Yoko Ono's "Walking on Thin Ice," Steve Miller's "Macho City," the Clash's "Lost in the Supermarket," or anything by Metal Urbain or Big Black). I love that one keyboard lick (doo de doo DOO, doo de doo DOO). Critics had given up on this guy as a total sellout by this point; sure the early solo stuff shows a lot more taste (especially *Gasoline Alley* and *Every Picture Tells a Story*), but the commerciality of this song doesn't ruin it for me, and never did. When you come right down to it, Jonathan Richman has turned his back on the truths of "A Plea for Tenderness" more decisively than Stewart has on "Maggie May" or "Every Picture Tells a Story."

In the July 1997 issue of *Alternative Press*, a list of ten essential Eighties new wave LPs (Duran Duran, Culture Club, Simple Minds, etc.) is titled "Was It Really That Bad?" Uh, that month's cover story was Veruca Salt, and Ben Folds Five and Supergrass were also profiled...like, are those bands any better? Looking at the issue in January 1999, the ad for a Bis record and the reference to the previous issue's Tool cover story already seemed hopelessly dated.

The Eagles, "The Long Run"
"I used to stay out till the break of the day/That just didn't get it/It was high time I quit it/I just couldn't carry on that way." I heard this after a week of partying till 5 a.m. and realized I had never heard the song as an adult (I was 11 when it came out). It's ironic that so much music aimed at "kids" deals with things they have no direct experience with. When I was 11, I wasn't partying till the break of day, that's for sure. As a kid, radio provided what I thought would be the soundtrack to adult life, listening to the radio was like going to an R-rated movie or something. But now as an adult, hit songs have little or no significance to me. In fact, it's obvious that because of oldies radio programming, the soundtrack to an adult's life is the same as the one to their teenage one, only it becomes nostalgia. The Sixties and Seventies hits that I heard growing up were the same songs that people in their twenties and thirties had listened to growing up, first hand. When I hear Gerry Rafferty's "Baker Street" and "Right Down the Line," Bob Welch's "Ebony Eyes," Donny Hathaway & Roberta Flack's "The Closer I Get to You," Raydio's "Jack and Jill," Dan Hill's "Sometimes When We Touch," Dan Hartman's "Instant Replay," Jackson Browne's "Running on Empty," Blondie's "Heart of Glass," or Al Stewart's "Time Passages," I remember being 10 years old, listening to Dan Ingram on WABC in New York on an old clock radio

in my room or in our car. Nobody who was 30 when those songs came out would hear them and say, "Oh yeah, I remember being 30 when that came out." Just like I won't really remember when Alanis Morrisette, Sheryl Crow, or Joan Osbourne had their hits (some of which I like, although I only hear them in passing). Sometimes, as a kid, pop music seemed like a substitute for experience, but it turns out to be an experience in itself, part of the experience of growing up, of the myth of adulthood.

DANCE HALL DAYS 2000:
A REASONABLE GUIDE TO HORRIBLE TASTE

All of the above encounters with Eighties music were by chance, and occurred in public spaces. However, in preparation for this book, I decided to re-experience more Eighties music via Rhino's loving and comprehensive fifteen-volume compilation series *Just Can't Get Enough: New Wave Hits of the Eighties*. I didn't slog through every track on all fifteen CDs, and tried to limit my listening to songs I remembered from back then. What was amazing was when certain songs would play that I didn't think I knew from the title that I would recognize immediately. Listening again I was struck by how much this stuff had influenced my songwriting and singing, especially in Love Child. I know the other people in Love Child knew all these tunes, and I know that many of our peers in indie rock (Mac MacCaughan, Lou Barlow, Lois Maffeo, Soo-Young Park, Kathleen Hanna, Mark Robinson) at the time (early Nineties) knew them too.

Haircut One Hundred, "Love Plus One"
I remember everything about this song as it plays. "Where does it go from here/Is it down to the lake I fear?/Ay yi yi yi yi yi/Ay yi yi yi yi YI yi yi." The first sax break is unfamiliar, but the chorus-ending "when I call—Luh-uh-VE!" and the weird phone voice saying "Here we go" before the second chorus both ring bells. As do the cymbals accenting the "ring and a/ring and a/ring and a/ring and a" in the second chorus. I barely remember the video for this, I think it's sort of summer-y with some nautical theme. I wonder what happened to Nick Heyward (the band's singer/songwriter)?

Toni Basil, "Mickey"

A novelty hit when it came out ('82, I reckon), I only remembered the cheerleader chant: "Hey Mickey you're so fine/You're so fine you blow my mind/Hey Mickey" before hearing it again, and of course the cheerleading video, shot against an all white backdrop. I remember every lyric as the song plays: "You think you got the right, but I think you got it wrong/'Cause when you say you will, it always means you won't/You're givin' me the chills, baby, please, baby, don't/Don't leave me in the jam, Mickey/Anyway you wanna do it, I'll take it like a man...." Etc., etc. Pretty old fashioned really, farfisa-driven, although the verse riff is derived from Gary Numan's "Cars." Toni was a choreographer and this was her only hit. I think the success of Laurie Anderson convinced some avant-garde types they could have a pop hit—and Toni did! More recently, I espied her in one of Bruce Conner's photographs of the original San Francsico punk scene circa 1978, looking totally wasted in a club (she also dances in his 1966 film *Breakaway* to one of her own early songs). I was also excited to see that Toni was one of the runaways in Bob Rafelson's classic 1970 film *Five Easy Pieces*, not to mention her appearances in *Easy Rider*, *The Last Movie*, and *Greaser's Palace*, which means she must have been in her early to mid-thirties when "Mickey" came out. Who knew?

Tim Curry, "I Do the Rock"

Another novelty hit, a real Roxy Music tribute musically with a lot of celebrity name dropping. Forgot most of this song, although the line about John and Yoko ("Sometimes they make love and art/inside the Dakota") had lodged in my subconscious somewhere. Curry was the star of *The Rocky Horror Picture Show* which I had lost all interest in seeing by the time I was old enough to actually go to a midnight screening.

The Inmates, "Dirty Water"
A remake of the old Standells tune that I used to hear on WPLJ a lot back in '79 or '80. Strangely, I remembered it as changing "Boston you're my home" to "New York you're my home," when in fact they sing "London you're my home." Kinda like someone I knew who remembered the wine in a scene in Hitchcock's *Strangers on a Train* being a certain shade of red when the film is in black and white! This brings up another point—the number of songs where I've heard the remake first, the original later. This includes all of *Abbey Road* (which I originally experienced on the *Sgt. Pepper* movie soundtrack), "Sister Ray" (heard Joy Division's live version on *Still* first), and Dylan's "Tangled Up in Blue" (heard Half Japanese's version first).

Talk Talk, "Talk Talk"
I remember the video listed the title three times, including the album title—I bet that really got J.J. Jackson's goat. I remember all the lyrics as it plays, and remembered the chorus beforehand. This song is alright, I guess. I was surprised to learn much later that they had gone on to make some cult art-song albums, like *Laughing Stock*, that Jim O'Rourke was quite enthusiastic about. They're no Music Machine, but who was back then?

Adam Ant, "Desperate But Not Serious"
Remembered each line as it played. This and "Ant Music" have a certain sinister quality that's a bit surprising for their ilk. The tremelo guitar line could've been played by Ira Kaplan as could the scraping guitar abuse at the end of the middle section (has anyone ever seen Ira and Marco Pirroni in the same room?). It's a drag that ex-punk Adam's pop success was so carefully calculated, but have you ever considered that "Adam Ant" and "adamant" are the same word? Very clever.

Culture Club, "I'll Tumble 4 Ya"
More ex-punks (the drummer even played in the Clash at one point) who went "pop"—and how. I'd never seen anyone like Boy George before, and with good reason—who'd want to look like that (a Hasidic/Kabuki/Kachina clown, that is)? Their combination of nancy-boy image and lite-calypso pop was practically toxic at the time, and though it's innocuous enough to me now, I still don't have much use for it. Although I guess I wouldn't mind hearing "Miss Me Blind" again someday....

Altered Images, "I Could Be Happy"
I remembered "Happy Birthday" better, but as this one played I recalled all the lyrics: "I could learn to climb/pine trees/I could be happy...all these things I do/to get away from you...get away/run away/get away, how do I/escape from you?" Lightweight and watery, but nevertheless a cleverly constructed pop song. Did anyone ever notice that Clare Grogan sounds a lot like Savage Rose's Annisette?

The Members, "Working Girl"
Hardly remembered this one, just the big boy's chorus, "Hey, I'm in love with a Working Girl," and the line "If she works 9 to 5/she oughta keep our love alive," and the cool chord behind "That's okay with me."

Naked Eyes, "What Do All the People Know?"
Only remembered the chorus before listening again, and it was still all I remembered. "All the people tell me so/but what do all the people know." A noble sentiment.

Rockpile, "Teacher Teacher"

I remember the intro guitar figure, but that's about it. Kind of pre–Stray Cats, roots-rock hopes, I think they broke up after one album. They had a good track on the *Concerts for Kampuchea* live LP (which provided a good representation of my taste in music at the time, come to think of it—the Who, Pretenders, McCartney, Clash, Costello…). I liked Dave Edmunds in Love Sculpture, and I'm down with Nick Lowe, but….

Robert Palmer, "Looking for Clues"

This used to be on MTV a lot—I could never figure out who this guy was, some solo guy with a record contract who never had any big hits. I would see ads for his records in music magazines but I never heard him until this song. And then he joined Power Station with some of the Duran Duran lads (their "rockist" side-project). What gives? I don't remember most of the lyrics as I hear this again, sorta remember the xylophone solo and the tap tap tap tap tap tap drum/synth thing, and the one line, "It's crazy but I'm frightened by the sound of the telephone/oh yeah." Not much of a song, I couldn't make it through.

Duran Duran, "Rio"

I know this one pretty well. I thought these guys were silly, but not as silly as some of their peers at the time and this is probably my favorite by them. Simon LeBon's vocal is mixed excruciatingly loud, like Courtney Love's on *Live Through This* (more on that later).

Sparks (with Jane Wiedlin), "Cool Places"

Forgot about this song completely, but remembered it really well as it played—alternating vocals, "Yeah I remember/last Saturday night/but I'm feeling cooler now/and they can tell we're cooler now/It's obvious we're cooler now, cooler now/cool cool cool, cool places with you" or "Then we'll sleep till 5 p.m./and start it up all over again/I never want to cool down, cool down/cool cool cool, cool places tonight." Like the show *Square Pegs* or the movie *Valley Girl*, this gets the school-misfits-out-on-the-town vibe just right. Jane was my least favorite Go Go after the fat one. (My favorite was Gina Shock—I think J.J. Jackson liked her too).

Psychedelic Furs, "Love My Way"

Remembered it instantly as that cool xylophone intro (shades of "Under My Thumb") kicked in. I recognized each line as it came out; "In a room without a door, a kiss is not enough...they just want to steal us all and take us all apart," and "If you don't run the race." "Race" goes off on a vocal tangent that's stolen right from the similar ending vocal of "Kid" by the Pretenders. I hear "Pretty in Pink" more often, but this is probably a better song. I've always liked Richard Butler's voice, he seemed like a guy who probably wanted to do harder-edged stuff but couldn't resist the brass ring (such as it was).

Echo & the Bunnymen, "The Cutter"

Didn't remember this one at all before it played. Then the Indian intro sounded familiar, and I remembered the melody and the lyrics as they went along—"Spare us the cutter," followed by that hard guitar chop, and those chorus lines, "I see another hurt approaching/ Say you can, say you will/Not just another drop in the ocean." And that weird, happier sounding coda.... I remember their live video of "Do It Clean/Sex Machine," which I dug—pretty energetic, but I never heard them other than that.

ABC, "Poison Arrow"

This and "The Look of Love" were their ultra fey hits. I only remembered the chorus of "Look" before and after listening to it again, but "Poison Arrow" became familiar again as it played on. The lyrics to this are pretty well-crafted, and it was nice to be reminded of that "You think you're smart/stupid, stupid" dunderhead line. This and pretty much everything else I've heard here reminds me of Roxy Music—Bryan Ferry's mannered vocals and image-consciousness and Andy MacKay's saxophone pretty much drew the blueprint for this entire pop movement. Minus Roxy's avant-garde edge of course, just as U.S. groups of the era like R.E.M. and the Violent Femmes took the jangle of the Velvets and dumped the avant-garde edge.

Kajagoogoo, "Too Shy"

The singer's name was Limahl—a first, I guess. I didn't care for this much at the time, and didn't remember much besides the chorus when I listened again—the verse melody was familiar but not the lyrics.

Heaven 17, "Let Me Go"

A pretty punk name for such a pansified band (taken from *A Clockwork Orange*). Sounds like Pavement copped some shit from the "ba ba ba ba ba ba ba da DA"s two and a half minutes in. Remember some of the lyrics—"guilty of no crime"—and the chorus, but this always struck me as mopey and a drag. Still, it's been in my head intermittently since I heard it again.

Thomas Dolby, "She Blinded Me With Science"
I always liked "Hyperactive," the follow-up hit, better than this. That one's a good Stevie Wonder rip-off, kinda like an electro "Superstition" at 78 rpm. Funny, I remember the incidental stuff in this song—the weird guy saying "Science," the munchkin backup vocals—more than the song itself, which is pretty flimsy to begin with, not really amounting to much more than the title. All these songs are too fucking long (this one's over four minutes!).

Thompson Twins, "Lies"
More good pop from three bad haircuts. I remember the opening keyboard line instantly, but not the lyrics. When he says "Japan" there's an Oriental motif underneath; when he says "Egypt" there's a snake charmer melody. Not too subtle, but it works. The bass line is stolen from "Low Rider" by War and the keyboard chords in the verse are lifted from "Spirits in the Material World" by the Police. I also remembered that "They're gonna get you!" during the break-down chorus, sounds like a party! Great stuff—as Johnny Carson used to say....

Haircut One Hundred, "Favorite Shirts (Boy Meets Girl)"
Duh, maybe McCartney should have called it "Scrambled Eggs (Yesterday)" (God, I'm such a geek). Hadn't given this one too much thought since '82, but remembered each line just before it happened whilst listening again, including the horn solos and the conga section. Did not recollect the faux rap section near the end, though. This was a likable band, in a hateful kind of way.

Split Enz, "Six Months in a Leaky Boat"
I remember "History Never Repeats" and "I Got You" more than this tune, especially considering I didn't remember it at all. The first line, "When I was a young boy," was familiar, everything after that wasn't. Oddly, this one was stuck in my head two weeks after playing it, an incredible delayed reaction. Supposedly this was banned by the BBC at the time, who misconstrued it as being about the Falkland Islands! Leader Neil Finn recently sold out the Bowery Ballroom here in New York—who is going to see this guy now???

Human League, "(Keep Feeling) Fascination"
Another one I blanked on until hearing it again. This repeats the boy/girl alternate singing of the League's first smash hit, "Don't You Want Me." At least that one had a he said/she said story line to hold your interest; this has lines like "And so the conversation turned/until the sun went down/and many fantasies were learned/on that day…Decisions to be made (hey hey-ay-hey HEY)/the good advice of friends are needed," etc. Weird microtonal synth riff too. This band was from Sheffield, as was the tour manager of a recent Papa M tour, who said that their guiding light Phil Oakey was still something of a local celebrity. Meanwhile, the Lester Bangs biography revealed that the poor galoot died listening to the *Dare* LP. Ouch…. I also once very meanly told a friend of mine, when asked if I had heard a certain record (can't remember what), that I had been listening to it "when you were still listening to the Human League." (He had previously admitted to being a devotee back in the day.) If you're reading this, I'd like to apologize.

The Call, "The Walls Came Down"

David Byrne sings the blues? I remember when this band came out I thought they might be cool, 'cause the name reminded me of the Alarm, and the Clash had a song named "The Call-Up" (I know, pretty questionable criteria), but they were lame. Didn't remember this being topical, thought it was on a Hootersian Christian trip, but check out these lines: "We got terrorists thinking/playing on fears...I don't think there are any Russians/and there ain't no Yanks." Yeah, yeah, and if you had a rocket launcher, some son of a bitch would die, correct?

A Flock of Seagulls, "Wishing (If I Had a Photograph of You)"

One of the worst looking of all these bands; the lead singer's blonde 'do was like some origami fantasia on a merkin. I don't think I ever knew this song by title, but I recognized it as soon as the opening synth line played. Some bad lines ("the way your eyes are laughing as they/gla-uh-ance"), but believe it or not, this is pretty majestic stuff. There's a Philip Glass–influenced mid-section, and the end, where they have big e-bow guitars arcing over the main riff, sounds like half of Yo La Tengo's back catalog (and some of Steve Reich's). This one stayed in my head for several days after replay; a classic of the era.

Naked Eyes, "Promises Promises"

Starts by ripping off Bowie's "Let's Dance," then it gets good. I remember the lyrics as it plays: "Never had a doubt/never a doubt...arm and arm we laughed like kids at/all the silly things we did/you made me/Promises, promises/knowing I'd believe...you knew you'd never keep," and the keyboard fills as they play too. I remember the last high note "Why do I be-LIEVE," just before it happens—the kid is hot!

Yaz, "Don't Go"
I turned to amazon.com for these next two—god bless them Real Audio samples! Remembered the synth line and the chorus of this one, nothing more. Kinda like the Eurythmics, only worse.

Howard Jones, "What Is Love?"
Another one where I draw a blank after the chorus, this guy seemed spineless at the time and doesn't come across as any more substantial now.

Big Country, "In a Big Country"
This was fairly exciting in '83, pretty pallid now, but then again I like bagpipes. I remember liking the subsequent single, "Fields of Fire" more. I'm a sucker for ScotRock—the first rock song I ever liked was "Saturday Night" by the Bay City Rollers, I'm into the Fire Engines, I think I saw the Pastels once, and that guy from Mogwai is really nice.

JoBoxers, "Just Got Lucky"
I like the chorus of this song, which stayed in my head for an extra day or two after hearing it again, and not much else—it's bad ska-pop with a Members-ish boys club vocal. The upright piano solo reminded me of the Neil Young one on Buffalo Springfield's "Burned," an allusion I'd wager is purely accidental. Turns out the lads are ex-punks too; according to Joe Carducci, some of Subway Sect wound up in this band.

Tears for Fears, "Change"
Back in the Seventies, Arthur Janov brought you the classic first John Lennon solo LP, in the Eighties he inspired these sissies. A sign o' the times? Decidedly. "Shout" was the big hit, couldn't take that one, the LP was called *The Hurting* (boo hoo). I remember the opening as it plays, but it must be in a car commercial or something 'cause I don't remember the rest at all. Okay, maybe the chorus, but barely.

DFX2, "Emotion"
I really liked this when it came out; to my more experienced adult ears, it's just an *Emotional Rescue*–era Stones rip, and not a real good one at that. The main guitar riff is PiL-like, and there's a cool, dissonant guitar solo (à la James Honeyman-Scott, let's not go crazy), too.

———————

July 20, 2000—I'm on the phone this afternoon, put on hold. The music playing is Peter Cetera's 1986 hit "The Next Time I Fall in Love." I'm sure if this song registered with me at all when it came out it was with contempt; I've long regarded his soppy e-z listening balladry, both solo and as the singer of Chicago, as insufferable. However, this song really connected with me today. There's one really stern chord change in the chorus that somehow belies the otherwise placid sentimentality of the tune, like a furrowed brow quickly giving way to a placid smile. I couldn't get it out of my head all day. That night I went to see the latest Glenn Branca symphony for ten guitars. It was one thirty-minute roar, all ecstatic high energy, a wash of overtones, very powerful. It should have been something I loved; I've been a fan and follower of Branca's work in the past, seen some of his other symphonies and liked them, and have consistently sought out overtone-based music and high energy guitar orgies, but I was totally bored by it. I concluded that I liked the Peter Cetera song much better than Glenn Branca.

How did I get to this point? I spent the better part of two decades unearthing alternatives to Peter Cetera (like Glenn Branca), rejecting the values of Peter Cetera, defining my life against Peter Cetera, but he will not be denied. Admittedly, I'm just not as interested in Branca as I used to be, probably wouldn't have bothered going if some friends weren't also on the bill, and compositionally, I thought the piece lacked a convincing structure. And yes, Branca's year beats Cetera's day. But that night I felt that a cycle in my life had ended. I felt it starting when I was no longer afraid to look at that picture of Joey Ramone, and when I went to see *Decline of Western Civilization* when it came out, just after seventh grade—seeing a tarantula crawl over Darby Crash's arm, hearing the singer of Black Flag say he lived in "a fucking closet," John Doe's "Fuck the World" tattoo, and oh yeah, the music, walking around Greenwich Village for the first time afterward, knowing right then I would opt out of my parents' and peers' conventional suburban lifestyles. I felt it starting to end when I heard "Hold Me Now" two years ago. Glenn Branca is no longer the good guy, Peter Cetera the bad. It's all just music.

Yes, I live my life with strangers
And the danger's always there
But when I hit Broadway and it's time to play
You know that I don't care
It's the New York City Rhythm runnin' through my life.

The poundin' beats of the city streets
That keeps my dreams alive
I'm lost, I'm found, I'm up and I'm down
But somehow I survive
It's got to be the New York City Rhythm in my life.

"New York City Rhythm," Barry Manilow, 1975

NOBODY KNOWS THAT I'M NEW WAVE

T-Shirt, mid-1990s

I.
IT'S GOT TO BE THE
NEW YORK CITY RHYTHM IN MY LIFE

I was 13 the first time I heard *The Velvet Underground & Nico* and it gave me a headache. But I continued to play it every day for the next three months. That started my love affair with New York rock, and New York itself, which was only 40 minutes away from Short Hills, New Jersey, where we lived. As a kid I'd bought into my parents' attitude of "It's a nice place to visit, but you wouldn't want to live there." My family would go to the theatre, or a museum, and then get the hell out. My mother had lived there for ten years before getting married, and would go back every chance she got, usually with me and my brother in tow. I always enjoyed these excursions, but throughout my childhood, I couldn't understand why anyone would want to live in an apartment and not a house with a backyard. That all changed. I got into the New York Dolls soon after, got the Ramones' *It's Alive* and Richard Hell's *Destiny Street* for my 14th birthday. I remember looking at the photo on the cover of *Destiny Street* of Hell playing bass on the bed in his apartment with his chick in the background, wanting a New York apartment of my own (I doubt that I had a concept of the East Village at that point). His guitarist, Robert Quine, also played with Lou Reed and became my New York guitar idol. In my mid-teens I once spotted him walking up Fifth Avenue; as a kid I kept wondering why I never ran into John and Yoko on the subway, so things were looking up. The original CB's/Max's scenes weren't that old back then, but already legendary. I picked up a copy of *NY Rocker*, the last issue, at my local record store, The Record Mill (in Millburn). The scene actually warranted its own monthly publication. I pored over the pages. (Cover story: "Hoboken: A Model Pop Community," with the Individuals and the Bongos; years later I would see the Individuals' Glenn Morrow taking his kids to school every day while I waited for the bus on Washington Street.) There was so much going on only 40 minutes from where I lived (but all after midnight). I would look at the ads in the *Village Voice* religiously, week after week, to see who was playing at CBGB's or Folk City, but I was still too provincial to really go to shows (driving into the city was beyond me). Hoboken had meant little to me other than the last stop on the commuter train before you changed to the PATH subway into Manhattan, but the *Rocker* piece hipped me to Maxwell's, which boasted a homegrown, underground rock atmosphere for urban tastes without the pretentions. I had a cousin living there, too, who loaned me Patti Smith's *Horses* (which is the Great American Novel, in case you never noticed) and a bunch of jazz albums. I'd read Robert Palmer's "Pop Life" column in the *New York Times* every week, where he would talk about all kinds of local music from Lydia Lunch to La Monte Young to Grandmaster Flash. His appreciation of everyone from Lydia to Duane Allman echoed my own, and he was very adroit at placing all of it in a continuum that was easy to relate to. Around 1985 he did a column called "Electric Guitars" where he talked about Glenn Branca, Sonic Youth, and Live Skull, and I immediately bought their records and the Tellus *All Guitars* cassette that they all appeared on. That cassette was a watershed for me, because it collected that whole scene, plus people like Elliott Sharp and Arto Lindsay, plus the Butthole Surfers, Blixa Bargeld, Steve Albini, and Bob Mould, making the connection between underground rock, noise rock, and downtown art music. I was also getting interested in the sort of stuff that New Music Distribution Service carried, heard a lot of it on Tim Page's afternoon music show on WNYC, and would go over to their loft at 500 Broadway once in a while and buy records, or order them by mail. Ranging from Philip Glass and Steve Reich–type stuff to Christian Marclay, Fred Frith, and other improvisors, they all lived in New York. I remember going to see Rhys Chatham at The Kitchen and standing behind Lee Ranaldo in line for the bathroom. I'd read Thurston Moore's open letter to Christgau in the Voice and I dug that Sonic Youth seemed to be into the same hardcore and rock bands I was into and stuff like Steve Reich and La Monte Young at the same time. I wanted to combine art music and rock music like them and Chatham and Glenn Branca, and the only place anyone seemed to be doing that was New York.

New York music had nothing to do with cock rock, boogie rock, the Grateful Dead, Styx, REO Speedwagon, Kansas—none of those bands ever came from New York. It was almost punk by definition. I was a big fan of *Cop* and *Raping a Slave* by the Swans. Those records were brutal and scary and seemed to define New York rock circa mid-Eighties for me. The four people on the back cover of *Cop* didn't look like people I'd want to hang out with, and that was cool. It was the same thing as that picture of Joey Ramone in *1988*—they looked threatening. When I got to college my freshman roommate had a copy of *No New York*, which was a revelation—this is where the Swans and Sonic Youth were coming from! The back cover was like a grid of mug shots, the "musicians" all looked like criminals, as did J.D. Daugherty holding a switchblade on the back cover of *Horses*, or the Ramones in their teenage gang getup. It would probably seem tame even to a teenager now, but to my very impressionable younger self it was intimidating—and exciting. I borrowed the first Suicide LP from a friend in college, the most assaultive New York group of them all. I would play "Frankie Teardrop" endlessly, which I rated right up there with *Taxi Driver* in terms of capturing the sense of violence and dread in Seventies' New York. The grindingly minimal music not only seemed to melt down Philip Glass and the Stooges into one, but to also replicate the industrial sounds of the city itself. And then there were the stories of actual violence by the performers at shows: Alan Vega from Suicide locking the doors of the Mercer Arts Center and lunging into the audience wielding a dagger; James Chance kicking a pregnant woman in the stomach (which prompted a physical attack on Chance by the *Voice*'s Robert Christgau); Lydia Lunch throwing her pick at a *NY Rocker* critic's glasses as a Teenage Jesus set ended; G.G. Allin's legendary anarchic gig at the Cat Club (witnessed by several of my friends at school).

Throughout college I kept reading the *Voice* and Gerard Cosloy's *Conflict* magazine, which kept me in touch with what was happening in the New York rock scene. Pussy Galore came out and they were big at the college radio station. We tried to get them to play but it never happened. They also looked like badasses (although in truth they were liberal arts students like us). In the summer of 1989, Rudolph Grey, who I'd first heard on the Tellus cassette and had interviewed on college radio and for *Black to Comm*, asked me to play bass with him and drummer David Linton in Thurston's Rock and Roll Circus, and a few months later Love Child, my band at school, played at CBGB's for the first time. I was finally taking part in the New York rock scene I had fantasized about for nearly ten years. Eventually, I met and played with many of the people who were on *No New York*, the people who were in the Swans, Quine—even went out with a woman who'd also dated Richard Hell (not the one on the cover of *Destiny Street*, though I've met her, too)—and joined a band with Rick Brown, who I had first seen pictured with V-Effect in that issue of *NY Rocker* some ten years earlier.

I recently watched the 1988 documentary *Put Blood in the Music* again. It has segments on Sonic Youth, John Zorn, Ambitious Lovers, Hugo Largo, and lots of talking heads like Lenny Kaye, Branca, Vernon Reid, Cosloy, and Lydia Lunch, all discussing the New York rock scene of the Seventies and Eighties. People were still talking about the sound of the subway and the energy of the streets influencing the music, all those clichés, but it was really true. The music was still aggressive and arty, and New York was still trashy, even as the Eighties art boom began to transform SoHo and rents in the East Village began to rise. At one point Karen Finley, the performance artist known for smearing her body with chocolate among other shock tactics, says something to the effect of we have to keep making art to keep the Upper East Siders out of the neighborhood (i.e., downtown). For a long time, they did. When the music was still noisy and violent, when the musicians still wore all black and had drug habits, this effectively scared away the squares. The streets weren't safe and the music reflected that.

So what happened in the Nineties? Rudy Giuliani became mayor and totally cleaned up the streets—of homeless people, of crime, of drinking beer on a stoop. It was practically martial law, but suddenly chains started opening here (Kmart, Starbucks), Avenue B became the site of boutiques and cafes instead of drug dens, 42nd Street went from all porno theatres to all Disney, and the East Village and SoHo were crowded with tourists all the time. TV shows like *Seinfeld* and *Friends* confirmed the idea that New York was now not only safe to visit, but to live in. A friend recently commented that people used to move to New York to hang out with Allen Ginsberg and Lou Reed, now they move here because they watch *Friends* (or, better yet, to watch *Friends* with Lou Reed!). Rents skyrocketed. When I arrived at junior high, high school, and even college, I was told that each used to be wild, but the new principal/dean was cracking down. Moving to New York (although just pre-Giuliani) continued this pattern.

And what were the bands of the Nineties in New York? Versus, Yo La Tengo, Magnetic Fields, Girls vs. Boys, Love Child, Sleepyhead, Chavez, Galaxie 500/Luna, Pony, Blonde Redhead, Railroad Jerk, Cell. None of them were junkies; hell, most weren't even drunks! They were suburban and a little sloppy, but essentially well-scrubbed. Some of them even played sports! Or wore Izod shirts. They were approachable after a show. Despite the use of distortion, their musical roots lay in New Wave, not No Wave. The music and attitude were not assaultive. Bob Bannister once typified this so-called "love rock" movement as "bands no one from Pussy Galore would ever go to see" (although Julie Cafritz saw Love Child a few times), while Ann Marlowe opined that these bands looked like they were going to the office when they got onstage (as opposed to Cop Shoot Cop, who trashed their gear after the first song). Codeine was as heavy and slow as the Swans, but melodic and normal looking. Two New York bands made inroads commercially: Helmet, who like Living Color before them proved that a CB's heavy metal band could have a hit, although unlike Living Color they started on an indie label (Amphetamine Reptile); and Soul Coughing, who stood firmly in the Talking Heads quirk rock tradition. D-Generation's members came out of the early Eighties hardcore scene and desperately aspired to be the new New York Dolls; if making two major label albums that nobody bought counts, they succeeded, otherwise they were more like Gotham's answer to Hanoi Rocks a decade too late. They also ran a club series called Green Door which was themed around the Seventies CB's/Max's scene, a noble sentiment but too retro to be relevant. Jonathan Fire*Eater rocked a better Dolls rip, but the singer's constant mugging was unbearable to watch onstage; as for their overall image, the Backstreet Boys drawn by Charles Addams might be one way of describing it. The Unsane and Surgery and Prong and all those other East Village scum rock bands had to be reckoned with, but most of them came out of the late Eighties just-post Pussy Galore scene and were essentially harmless.

Speaking of which, where were the Eighties bands? Lydia Lunch moved out. The Swans redid a Joy Division song and got on MTV. Jon Spencer formed the initially powerful but ultimately cartoonish Blues Explosion. Neil Hagerty and Jennifer Herrema's Royal Trux were originally in the New York noise tradition, somewhat, but moved around the country and have emerged as the true inheritors of the Meat Puppets' vision of fucked up classic rock (or is that classic fucked up rock?). Arto Lindsay concentrated on Brazilian sounds and production, then rediscovered skronk in the grunge era. The Feelies broke up (again). So did Das Damen. White Zombie became best-selling major label metallers. Jim Foetus signed to Sony, was dropped before he could even finish a tour behind the album, and has been keeping a low profile ever since.

Sonic Youth signed to a major label and sang about crème brûlée and free time as opposed to Sadie Mae Glutz or complete inhumans. Savage Pencil recalls going to interview them in the mid-Eighties thinking, "They were going to be vicious, mean mofos from NYC—they'd be digging up dead bodies. When I got down there they were goofy, really friendly." That was crucial. Sonic Youth took music with titles like "Ghost Bitch" out of the goth arena. They got lumped in with the industrial crowd early on but unlike Psychic TV or whomever, they weren't trying to come off as anti-social freaks. They sounded weird but they looked and acted pretty normal. This makes them pivotal in the Eighties-to-Nineties New York scene. They continue to set an example for younger groups, and a good one, too, both as an autonomous band operating on a major label (practically a law unto themselves, really) and as consistent supporters of terminally obscure music (what other band in their position would have taken the Dead C. on tour with them in 1995?). Still, as they approach their twentieth year together, they seem more relevant as a NYC institution, like Allen Ginsberg or Andy Warhol, than as a "band."

CBGB's still had a good booking policy in the early Nineties, but more recently has been home to an endless supply of shitty bar bands, usually five to seven a night. Maxwell's was still a good hangout when I moved to Hoboken in 1991, but with less and less musicians living in Hoboken, the closing of Pier Platters (a great record store that made the trip to Hoboken more worthwhile for New Yorkers), and the general commercial ascendancy of the music it catered to, it lost a lot of lustre by the mid-Nineties. Unpretentious to a fault, it was definitely the place to see the Gories or Hasil Adkins (or even something like the Chills or Superchunk), but anything artier than the Feelies felt out of place there, because of both the atmosphere (very no-frills) and the sound system (ditto). It closed for awhile after a disastrous change in ownership, but recently reopened.

It seems more and more likely that the CB's/Max's scene of the mid- to late-Seventies, whose influence was still felt through the entirety of the Eighties, was much like the Athens scene of the early Eighties, or the Seattle scene of the late Eighties—a spontaneous combination of people and cheap rents in a specific time and place that produced a rock scene that was hyped as the next big thing, and then mined by the media and major labels, which of course ruins it. Despite the Dylan/Lou Reed/Fillmore East Sixties legacy, New York is not a rock and roll town. Most of the classic New York bands were cult bands made up of artists or writers who drifted into rock. The increasing lack of coverage of the local scene in the *Voice* or *New York Press* parallels the onslaught of corporate culture in Manhattan. Covering national acts at the expense of local ones is similar to shopping at Borders or Starbucks instead of St. Mark's Books or Limbo (of course, both papers consistently lament the rise of chain stores in lower Manhattan).

As the neighborhoods became friendlier, so did the bands. As the streets became safer, so did the music. Or was it the other way around? Not that the music was necessarily bad—a lot of it is great. But what does it have to do with New York? Just as the onset of malls, multiplexes, chain retail outlets, and the like threaten New York's anti-hick identity, the New York rock scene's anti-hick identity has eroded too. Just like New Yorkers are no longer thought of as rude or cold, New York music isn't that way either.

II.
THE CLINTONIZATION OF ROCK

I knew the Eighties were over when I saw Pavement at Maxwell's in 1990 (opening for either Babes in Toyland or the Smashing Pumpkins, I don't remember which, but I was there to see Pavement). Those guys dressed like preppies but played shambling music. I knew preppies over the years who liked punk rock, including another one of my cousins, but I'd never seen a band dressed like that playing onstage (consider Julie Cafritz's clothes in Pussy Galore and in the post-Pavement Free Kitten). Stephen Malkmus may have owed a sonic debt to the Fall, Sonic Youth, and Swell Maps (especially in the beginning), but when interviewed he'd compare the band to Steely Dan (commercial but twisted) and, memorably, to Seventies prog also-rans Barclay James Harvest. Polvo went them one better by sounding like Sonic Youth but dressing like they were off to soccer practice after the gig!

And I knew the Eighties were over when Dinosaur covered Peter Frampton's "Show Me the Way" (which doesn't sound out of place with the rest of their '87 repertoire). Instead of being about the Sixties this was Seventies revisionism and not done as a parody. Around the same time I saw Todd Haynes's *Superstar*, a 45-minute biopic of Karen Carpenter that legitimately established her, and the decade that produced her, beyond kitsch as a tragic icon. Friends of mine at college were already doing an all-Seventies hits radio show. I distinctly remember going to an all-hipster party my freshman year (1986) where the entire *Saturday Night Fever* soundtrack album was played (although the host, future Go Ahead Booking agent Ellen Stewart, does not remember this). People disparaged the Seventies in the Seventies. It was the Me Decade, known for what was considered poor fashion sense, Watergate, defeat in Vietnam, disco, and general tackiness. It was seen as a big comedown from the Sixties, not the golden age people seem to consider it now. If the Eighties were about trying to relive the Sixties, and the Seventies about reviving the Fifties (from *Sha Na Na* to *Happy Days* and *American Graffiti* to the Ramones' leather jackets and Bryan Ferry's hair), the Nineties were about trying to relive the Seventies, whether it was Brady Bunch movies, 8-track fanzines, Urge Overkill's clothes, Quentin Tarantino, etc. But beyond the nostalgia/kitsch value, there were some important aesthetic reparations being made with Seventies artists who went into eclipse in the Eighties. The best that the decade had to offer was mined extensively in the Nineties. People like Neil Young and Robert Altman, who had both done a series of idiosyncratic and naturalistic genre exercises that spoke for an entire generation in the Seventies, and pretty much sleepwalked through the Eighties, made resounding comebacks in the early Nineties (Altman's *The Player* and *Short Cuts*, Young's *Ragged Glory*). John Fahey, whose staggering acoustic guitar extrapolations of the Sixties and Seventies were largely forgotten in the wake of the noxious waxings of the Windham Hill label in the Eighties, was rediscovered by a new generation. The minimalism of Philip Glass, Steve Reich, Terry Riley, Tony Conrad, Phill Niblock, and Charlemagne Palestine, which had somehow gotten lumped together with new age music in the Eighties, found a new audience, its credibility restored. Miles Davis's mid-Seventies recordings, which were ignored at the time for being too scabrous, bleak, and bombastic, were suddenly reissued and re-appreciated. The films of John Cassavetes, scorned in their day for being "indulgent" and "unprofessional," were suddenly fashionable and influential.

The people responsible for all this were born in the Sixties and remembered the Seventies, but barely. I thought Watergate was some building in D.C. that had a big flood (I was 6 at the time). I dimly recall *Jaws* opening, and staying up till 8 to watch *Happy Days* was a special occasion. I was just in time for *Star Wars* and *Animal House*, Jimmy Carter, the original *Saturday Night Live*, and disco and punk (I first saw the Sex Pistols on CBS's Saturday morning news spot "In the News" in between cartoons). The so-called Generation X for which I qualified was, like "hippie," a term concocted by the media, but it did exist. When Joan Baez congratulated a Live Aid audience with "This is your Woodstock and it's long overdue," she was way off base. Lollapolooza was the new Woodstock, and Generation X were the new hippies. Then again, consider the images of all those bands covered in mud at Woodstock '94—a perfect visual metaphor for the "grunge" era in its most positive light, a genuine punk-derived rethinking of the rock performer's identity. At the original festival, the stars were nowhere near any mud. Trent Reznor playing an entire set caked in dirt is pretty punk, I gotta say.

I remember buying my first indie album, the Minutemen's *What Makes a Man Start Fires?* when it came out (1982), and looking at the labels on the record. One side listed all the songs, the other was a Raymond Pettibon drawing of two Confucian figures, with the caption "Fuck As Holy." That seemed so much cooler than, say, the Epic logo, that for years after I avoided any major label LP in general, but especially those by ex-indie bands (Hüsker Dü, X) on principle—as an SST bumper sticker put it, CORPORATE ROCK STILL SUCKS. And those bands never hit big commerically. Nirvana was the first to go the distance. And how did they do it? By incorporating hit influences from both AOR and college radio (Pixies, R.E.M., Boston, the Beatles) along with the usual indie ones (Sonic Youth, Sabbath, Dinosaur, Black Flag).

How did Bill Clinton get elected? The same way Nirvana did. By taking the rising liberalism of the time and cutting it with conservativism (for every lefty issue he was behind, like gays in the military or pro-choice, there was one like a ratings system for network television). DJ Spooky once told me he thought that Clinton remixed politics. I thought that was a good way of putting it. Nirvana remixed punk, college radio, and classic rock radio. People like Hüsker Dü, Dinosaur, and the Replacements (among others) had been starting to do it for years, just not as brazenly and as successfully. Riot Grrrls remixed feminism by simultaneously embracing and re-imagining female stereotypes. In each of these cases, the dichotomies collapsed. Before Nirvana, alternative rock meant something that wasn't ready for the mainstream. After Nirvana, it *was* the mainstream. In the Eighties, no alternative band worried about writing catchy tunes, it was all about how fucked up you could be, how far from corporate rock you could be—look at the efforts of the Butthole Surfers, Meat Puppets, Half Japanese, Big Black, etc., in the mid-Eighties. There was a separate sub-genre, "pop-punk," like the Descendents or the Eastern Dark, but it was regarded as Ramonesian and not a bid for commerciality. Even melodic bands like Hüsker Dü or the Replacements distanced themselves from the mainstream either through sheer velocity, screamed vocals, and guitar noise (Hüskers), or by sloppiness bordering on pure anarchy (the 'Mats). When I wrote "Know It's Alright" for Love Child, I was stealing from both Olivia Newton-John's "Have You Never Been Mellow" and Red Transistor's "Not Bite." In the Nineties you had to be catchy and somehow "weird" or sloppy. The success of lo-fi pop like Sebadoh, Guided By Voices, Liz Phair, Smog, and Pavement exemplifies this. When Love Child did our demos on a four-track in March 1988, the term lo-fi didn't exist. The band's founding member, Will Baum, was the first person I knew who owned one—I thought they were just a toy for people like Nile Rodgers to fool around with at home, it didn't occur to me that normal folks could do something real with them. Later, when the demos came out as a single and we started playing shows outside of school with bands like Beat Happening and Sebadoh (who also traded instruments and vocalists depending on whose song it was, like we did) and Pavement and Superchunk (who were also recording lo-tech pop) I realized we were part of a movement. Before that I thought we were just dorks.

The changeover to popularity wasn't easy. Nirvana appeared on the cover of *Rolling Stone* with Cobain sporting a T-shirt on which he scrawled CORPORATE MAGAZINES STILL SUCK. I remember hearing about him going to see the Melvins and kids taunting him about being a sell-out, a member of "the B-52s" or something (just as Clinton was sometimes accused by liberals of pandering to the Right); and later Jello Biafra (who was never on a major label) was badly beaten at a show for the same alleged offense. It took me months just to buy My Bloody Valentine's *Loveless* even after being blown away by them live, simply because it was on a major label (so how good could it be?).

It got pretty gross pretty quick. You had bands like Afghan Whigs or Urge Overkill, typical indie bands turned AOR wannabes. You had Pearl Jam and Soundgarden, who were always neo-AOR to me, I could never figure out why they were in college radio-land to begin with. You had the Lemonheads, who formed inspired by the Angry Samoans, became a Replacements soundalike band, and then a best selling college rock band with leader Evan Dando enjoying some pinup appeal as a virtual Gen X David Cassidy (or "alterna-hunk," as was said at the time). I'd met Evan around 1986, not long after the Lemonheads started, because several of his high school friends had become friends of mine at college. The Lemonheads came down and played a set of all Black Sabbath covers there once. I always liked Evan; he was kinda vapid but sweet. He was the first person I knew to become a "star." Soul Asylum started in Minneapolis in the mid-Eighties primed to be the next Hüsker Dü or Replacements (Hüsker's Bob Mould produced them early on). They somewhat predictably signed to a major and then out of nowhere had a hit single in the early Nineties. Their leader, Dave Pirner, ditched his long-time girlfriend and went out with Winona Ryder. When he couldn't follow up the hit, she split. I remember hearing a couple of years ago they couldn't even sell out a show at Maxwell's.

You also had Sub Pop signing forgettable pop bands like Velocity Girl. I saw them at Maxwell's, pre–Sub Pop, opening for the 3Ds and didn't even remember them playing the next day. A couple of years later I opened up a copy of *Billboard* to see an article on them where the guitarist was talking about how radio-ready their new album was, how it was pure pop and not alternative. You could practically see the dollar signs in his eyes. In the same issue, Slayer talked about how they handed in their new album to the record label, who complained that there were no radio-friendly tracks. The band told them that they would be happy to go back to the studio to come up with more material, but it wasn't going to get any more commercial than what they'd already handed in. That really summed up the times for me.

And you had punk rock yuppies like Billy Corgan and Courtney Love. Billy may have liked to wear a T-shirt with ZERO written on it, but he was always looking out for Number One. Corgan told *Spin* magazine that, unlike Kim Gordon (or Nirvana), he liked playing for jocks and told Charlie Rose that the Pumpkins always aspired to be a big band, not a cult phenomenon like Alex Chilton. Yet they came up through the indie circuit—they put out their own single and played Maxwell's and CBGB's—Loverboy didn't do that. In other words, Corgan tried pot, but he never inhaled. Hole's epochal *Live Through This* is a great album, but not because they're a great band— it's because Courtney makes such a great case for herself as a rock star on it. She's as good a lawyer/politician as Hillary Clinton on that album, a brilliant 40-minute campaign. The vocals are pushed to the max in the mix, leaving the rest of the band in the dust; the songs are very post-Nirvana (putting it charitably), tuneful, sing-songy, and raucous at the same time, perfectly in step with the times. Just to keep the purists happy, and to show hipsters she didn't start listening to this stuff yesterday, there's a cover of a Young Marble Giants tune. Hole also started off playing CB's (I saw them there; Thurston's take that night was, "They sound like Eight-Eyed Spy," which was pretty dead-on) and recording for Caroline but not for long as Courtney put on her presidential kneepads, snared the Negative (Big) Creep and went into high gear. Thurston's comment is especially ironic when you consider that Lydia Lunch told *Forced Exposure* that what made her stop doing Eight-Eyed Spy "was popularity—that's just too boring. It grossed me out. Hate me, just don't love me in that way. I hate to be loved because it's the time to love me. There's nothing worse."

My own band, Love Child, had a meeting with Tim Sommer of Atlantic Records based on the fandom of Kurt Cobain who'd allegedly told Danny Goldberg we could be the next Fleetwood Mac and wanted to produce us. I could believe it, because Thurston had introduced me to Courtney Love at Maxwell's a year or two before.

When he said I was in Love Child, her eyes widened and she gasped, "He's So Sensitive!" (one of our more popular songs). I just rolled my eyes—that pretty much ended the conversation. I'm told Cobain also owned a self-made Love Child painter's cap. Maxwell's was also the site of our showcase gig for Tim's benefit; this was auspicious because Sommer was a former Hoboken resident who'd put in a lot of time at the club. ("It was the first place I saw R.E.M.," he told us in hushed tones, as if it had been the Beatles at the Cavern.) Although I've never wanted to work for any kind of corporation, I was willing to consider it, but nothing ever came of it; nobody was pushing for it on a managerial level, and not long afterward Cobain died, Sommer (a member of Hugo Largo and a former Glenn Branca sideman, natch) had signed Hootie and the Blowfish, and the rest, as they say, is history. I read an article about the Melvins a year or two later, who got a similar deal with Atlantic with Kurt producing. Cobain was apparently nodding out continually during recording sessions, and Atlantic released a couple of records without much fanfare. The band felt that the deal had secured their future as a touring act, but was otherwise disappointing to say the least.

Now when you turn on the TV and hear the Stooges and the Buzzcocks in car commercials, it's really hard to remember how new this game was. Just like the Democrats had always been defeated by Reagan and then Bush, it seemed like there was no commercial potential for this stuff. The original punk bands all had their major label albums come out in the Carter presidency (another Democrat) and they all stiffed. In high school I was considered a weirdo for liking the Ramones. Ten years later, Green Day had a million-selling album that essentially sounded like *Road to Ruin*. Suddenly everything was potentially marketable, potentially commercial. Suddenly some of the most fucked up bands of the Eighties—Sonic Youth,

Butthole Surfers, Mike Watt, Redd Kross, Royal Trux, Meat Puppets—were on major labels. Early Eighties SoCal hardcore bands like Social Distortion and Bad Religion made successful comebacks on major labels. Bad Religion's Epitaph label, now with major label distribution, had a hit with the Offspring. Chumbawumba, a long-running part of the U.K. Crass punk scene, had a top ten hit out of nowhere ("Tubthumping"). Suddenly you could read about all these bands in *Rolling Stone* (whose publisher Jann Wenner had rejected the Sex Pistols album as the critics poll winner in 1977 and substituted Fleetwood Mac's *Rumors* instead). I met a writer from *Rolling Stone* in a bar once several years ago; he knew the Love Child albums and asked what I was doing now. I told him I'd just recorded a 20- minute version of a Minutemen song; he'd never heard of the Minutemen (he's somewhat older than I am). A couple of months later, he wrote a review of a Mike Watt album (the one with Eddie Vedder and lots of other Nineties celebs on it) which proclaimed the Minutemen one of the best bands of the Eighties....

It trickled down to the fringes, too. Perennial fanzine cult favorites like Ohioans Jim Shepard and Ron House got inked to a specially created "indie" subsidiary of Def America (which should have been called "Def Sweden" but wasn't...). Lou Barlow's Folk Implosion had a Top 40 hit. Beck transcended his unwitting low budget slacker anthem "Loser" to become a bona fide entertainer who retained some musical credibility. By the end of the decade his shows were practically one-stop shopping for the aging hipster—a little folk, a little punk, Seventies threads, a lot of hip-hop. (Radiohead has also survived one-hit-wonderdom to provide similar one-stop service for a mopier constituency raised on angst-ridden guitar rock and *The Wall* but swayed by electronica, too.) Thurston showed a Harry Pussy video on MTV, and suddenly their LP sold out in an afternoon. The Frogs, a genuinely gifted songwriting team from Milwaukee with scores of homemade cassettes and a penchant for taboo lyric matter that made them controversial even in the supposedly free-thinking hipster ghetto (and good costumes, too), opened for Pearl Jam and even joined Smashing Pumpkins at one odd juncture. Even Daniel Johnston, a mentally unstable lo-fi Eighties pioneer, had an Elektra contract waiting for him if he could keep his illness in check enough to satisfy the suits (he couldn't). It was exciting, but ironically alienating. In the Eighties there was a cartoon by Jim Ryan called "The Low Life Scum" which brilliantly lampooned the sort of bohemian dorks who scoured thrift stores for Leonard Nimoy LPs and wore Converse high tops; somehow the youth culture became entirely populated by these creatures. A *Time* magazine cover story headline at the time read "Everybody's Hip (and That's Not Good)." For the first time I felt like my personal taste was generational taste, for the first time I felt part of a demographic. In some ways you could interpret this as a reward for "fighting the good fight" in the Eighties (as it was for people like Henry Rollins, Mike Watt, or Sonic Youth, who had been touring relentlessly long before an indie venue circuit or booking agencies had been established) or some such shit, but it actually depressed me to think that millions of other people liked this crap too. In the Eighties, when you met someone who knew and gave a fuck who the Minutemen or Flipper or Minor Threat were, it was special, because you had to seek that scene out, it wasn't handed to you by the mass media. You had to go beneath the surface. It was us vs. them. One of the great fanzines of the period was *Forced Exposure*, a hulking 100-plus page compendium of underground culture delivered with expertise and sharp, defiantly anti-PC humor. Reading *Forced Exposure* cover to cover armed you against the prevailing tastes of the Reagan era, but left you ill-prepared for the year punk broke—

it thrived on the us vs. them mentality. In a way, it's not surprising that they stopped publishing in 1993. A couple of years earlier, *F.E.*'s Byron Coley's "Underground" column in *Spin*, which covered a lot of the same ground as he did in *F.E.* in a more digestible, monthly form, had been cancelled due to publisher Bob Guccione Jr.'s conviction that the underground didn't exist. (Coley spent one final, hilarious column looking for the underground, since Bob told him the column could stay if he could prove the underground's existence.)

Since liking indie rock no longer made me a freak, I had to start listening closer to free jazz, modern classical, and psychedelic folk (all of which, coincidentally, had been showing up increasingly in *Forced Exposure*'s pages). That became the same thing—if you found somebody who had a bunch of old ESPs or BYGs or listened to Keiji Haino or Charles Gayle, it was cool. Eventually my generation latched on to that stuff, too, but never in the numbers approaching the membership of grunge America (or before them, the Kiss Army).

In the Eighties it was us vs. them—the U.S. vs. Communism. You know, the Cold War, the "Evil Empire." Once Gorby dissolved the Soviet Union, once the Berlin Wall came down, etc., etc., it was all over for the Republicans. You don't need those guys building nuclear arsenals to protect you anymore. You don't feel insecure about the Iranian hostage crisis or losing Vietnam anymore. You don't have to run back to the "family values" of the Fifties 'cause you think maybe too much social freedom in the Seventies wasn't such a good thing after all. The nonsense fantasy of nuclear destruction and Star Wars defense shields that distracted people from the very real social ills outside and inside their own walls had dissipated. So the road was clear to "be real." And what better way than with feedback and flannel shirts? Punk/indie had been real all along, that was the appeal. The people who liked it hadn't bought into the Republican values of the Eighties. But now that nobody was buying into that anymore, it became mass appeal. In a way the success of Nirvana and the election of Bill Clinton was just a big celebration for the end of the Cold War. We can think about real issues again 'cause nobody's gonna drop the bomb on us. We can listen to real music again. The Eighties were a reactionary, dark time, completely ruled by fear.

To me, the film *Terminator* really captures the feeling of that decade. In it, a cyborg from a post-nuclear-apocalyptic future (played by Arnold Schwarzenegger in a career-defining role) travels back through time to 1984 L.A. to catch the Olympics—no, just kidding—to kill the mother of a freedom fighter before she conceives him. One of the rebel's followers also travels to 1984 to protect her life. He explains the machine-man she's up against: "It can't be bargained with, can't be reasoned with, doesn't feel pity, or remorse, or fear, and it will not stop—ever." The creature he's describing is, subtextually, Ronald Reagan. He won't bargain with terrorists, cannot be reasoned with that Star Wars will never work or that his economic strategies aren't working, doesn't feel pity or remorse for the massive unemployment or budget cuts of social services during his administration, is not afraid of nuclear war or the USSR or Libya or anybody, survives an assassination attempt, wins by a landslide in both terms of office and surely would have been elected to a third term if possible—he will not stop, ever. In some ways Reagan's massive approval ratings could be read as a country afraid that if we disapproved of him he'd push the button and blow us all to kingdom come—remember the "bombing starts in five minutes" bit? Like the *Twilight Zone* episode "It's A Good Life", in which a monstrous little boy who can read minds can wish those who think "bad thoughts" or displease him in some other way into a cornfield forever or turn them into a "grotesque, walking horror" like a human jack-in-the-box. So an entire town tells him, "You did good, it was good that you did that," no matter what atrocity he perpetrates on their friends and neighbors. "He moved an entire community into the dark ages, just by using his mind," Rod Serling says in the episode's introduction. It was remade in *Twilight Zone: The Movie*—released a year before *Terminator*.

Iran-Contra was the first crack in the veneer. Then the Wall Street crash in '87. Then the Berlin Wall comes down. Then the Gulf War comes and goes. Then you had the Anita Hill case. Nobody seemed to believe her at the hearings, but all you heard about for the next few years was sexual harrassment and an increased sensitivity to same. *Thelma and Louise*, the Mike Tyson and O.J. trials, and Susan Faludi's *Backlash* also brought more discussion about women's issues. Pretty soon after *Twin Peaks* there was increased sensitivity to and awareness of incest, with people (some of them celebrities) talking about it from personal experience. This was when the term "dysfunctional family" came into parlance, when people started really opening up about how fucked up their family was or had been (the fall 1991 issue of the literary journal *Granta*, themed around The Family, was titled "They Fuck You Up"). TV comedies like *Roseanne* or *The Simpsons* couched some harsh truths about how families really operated. People were much more vocal in their offense taken to various minority stereotypes. "Happy Kwanzaa" took its place alongside "Happy Hanukkah" and "Merry Christmas." Political correctness became an obsession (terms like African-American and Asian replaced Black and Oriental about this time, not to mention Ebonics for, um, jive). Diversity and multiculturalism were the new values. Suddenly cock rock didn't make it anymore. Even a transitional band like Guns N' Roses, who had some punk influences in their hair metal (and choice of T-shirts—Axl or somebody wears a CB's one in one of their early videos), seemed stodgy and out of touch compared to Nirvana (much like George Bush to Bill Clinton). Alternative rock was just part of an emerging alternative social fabric based on extreme sensitivity that was, in fact, over-compensating for the greed, selfishness, and callousness of the Eighties. For all the ludicrous trends of the time—grunge designer clothes and the like—I have to say I'll take that over the cultural void of the Eighties anyday.

Grunge was just the musical entertainment at the Cold War/Reagan-Bush/Bush-Qualyle wrap party. And it *was* a celebration. I'll never forget being at a party on election night 1992 on Waverly Place in the West Village. As soon as it was announced that Clinton had won, not only did the room erupt into applause, but you could hear the same thing happening in every apartment building on the block, and down in the street. The Eighties were finally over. Everyone there was in their early twenties and had lived their entire adolescence in Reagan's America; now young adulthood would be spent in Clinton's America. Clinton was a recombinant President, equal parts Reagan-teflon, Jefferson-Southern lawyer with a sax instead of a violin, Carter family (Roger and Chelsea = Billy and Amy), Kennedy sex symbol/Camelot, and FDR visionary/adulterer. Like a song that reminds you of three or four other songs (such as "Smells Like Teen Spirit"), or a band that sounds like several classic bands, Clinton was a comforting pastiche of the familiar. His mass appeal was equivalent to that of a rock star like Springsteen or Bono—someone who gives the impression that he's just like his audience but also towering heroically above it. His weaknesses for fast food, extramarital sex, and stretching the truth gave him a set of bonding tools with the great unwashed. Joe Eszterhas and Oliver Stone may grumble that the Clintons showed Boomers at their worst, but frankly, their elders, Reagan and Bush, a pair of former liberals who both did an ideological flip-flop, were far more representative of how the Eszterhas/Stone generation turned out (no wonder Neil Young and Dennis Hopper voted for them). Clinton may have been sleazy, but at least he was *always* sleazy.

I went to see Pizzicato Five around 1995 at Irving Plaza, and they had a video running the whole time of clips of the *Pink Panther* and 007 films and all kinds of fun stuff like that, brilliantly edited together. In the Reagan/Thatcher days, PiL played behind a video screen, and Psychic TV had a video during their show of Jim Jones, Charles Manson, and penis piercing. Yuk. Who wants to see that gruesome, shocking stuff when there's no Nancy Reagan or Moral Majority to affront or when nuclear apocalypse ain't just around the corner (or, arguably, even if it is). I think the aggressive or assaultive rock performances of yore were aimed at the repressive nature of the times (remember, the Republicans were in office during the Stooges' and G.G. Allin's lifespans). There was no reason to assault the audience in the Nineties, 'cause we were all on the same page—after all, Clinton's an Elvis/Fleetwood Mac/Coltrane fan. It took all the fun out of hating the government. Consequently, whatever efforts were made to transform society were done by whining rather than assaulting, a sort of cultural nitpicking that encompassed everything from litigation over the temperature of spilt coffee to the sexual orientation of *Sesame Street* characters. Kurt Cobain never said anything about wanting to destroy passersby, he just had a new complaint. This was a secret meaning of slacking—opting out of "protest" as just another boomer cliché. Saying that Thanksgiving is a racist holiday doesn't involve as much personal risk as, say, crusading for civil rights did in the early Sixties. Iggy's stage antics in the early Seventies had at least a spiritual kinship with the student rioters of the time— there was a willingness to put your own body on the line for something you believed in. That sort of commitment didn't exist in the Sub Pop era, which is part of why that music is just a pale echo of the Stooges. This collective social semi-responsibility also gave the media the impression that we're more interested in the O.J. trial, the death of Di, or whatever sexual escapades are transpiring in the current executive administration, than in actual issues or events. It seems to be shifting now—kids are no longer lounging around in nirvanas and soundgardens, they're feeling rage against the machine. Not that that makes for better music—way worse, in fact....

Part of the excitement was seeing what and who your generation really was. It was the first time there was any focus on my age group—before that the baby boomers and yuppies got all the attention. Working part time, playing in an "alternative band," wearing thrift store duds that gave me an uncomfortable resemblence to Shaggy on Scooby Doo—superficially, I guess, I fit the typical slacker/generation X/hipster-doofus stereotype. I think part of why people lose interest in new rock as they get later into their twenties is that they've already seen what their generation is going to come up with—it speaks for them at that moment in the early twenties when they haven't settled down yet, then they get distracted by other things. At one point a publicist at Matador informed me that rock had died in 1983—roughly when the original punk/indie scene of her youth had died out. This really illustrates the point—people her age weren't forming bands any more, so she lost interest. Of course, that doesn't mean it died. People are always pronouncing some art form or another dead when its cultural moment passes, or as they get older, or when their tastes change.

———

I knew grunge was over when I heard the first Tortoise album at a party. I thought it was an old Herbie Hancock fusion album. Visiting their loft on Run On's first trip to Chicago, I saw a huge painting of John Coltrane on the wall and some dudes jamming in the back that sounded like Santana. I remember John Herndon opening their fan mail and getting letters from kids saying they were getting into jazz because of listening to Tortoise. The band succeeded in referencing music from outside their audience's listening parameters (Adrian Sherwood, Ry Cooder soundtracks, Augustus Pablo, Steve Reich, Zappa, Weather Report) and making those influences hip. It wasn't indie power trios any more either—Tortoise had two bassists, vibes, two drummers, a percussionist, and synths. For me the turning point was 1995, the one year Lollapolooza had mostly good bands on it (S.Y., Hole, etc.) and tanked; it was also when the whole DJ/remix/techno/dub explosion started to happen. This sort of pendulum swing was inevitable, but the timing was also similar to that of the mid- to late-Eighties instrumental bands that evolved out of the hardcore scene (Blind Idiot God, Gone, Universal Congress Of, DOS). Mind you, there had been plenty of antitheses to grunge that were popular during its time—ambient techno, Krautrock, and the lounge revival. But I don't think it was a reaction to grunge like pop art was to abstract expressionism, or minimalism was to serialism. If anything, it may be like fusion's emergence out of hard bop in the late Sixties and early Seventies. Or psychedelia's emergence out of British Invasion/garage/folk rock; just as Jerry Garcia shed his jugband to electrify/acidify with the Dead, so did DJ Spooky, Moby, and Fennesz leave behind their conventional bands (Spooky was a bassist, Moby played in Connecticut hardcore faves the Vatican Commandos, Fennesz played guitar in rock bands) in order to go electronic—and significantly, solo. It's interesting how many of these acts are either solo or duos, as opposed to a band unit—it's part of the true break with rock culture. You could take the psychedelic comparison further; that when Quicksilver or the Dead were extending "Who Do You Love" or "Dancing in the Street" into half-hour opuses, they were essentially remixing them. In the mid-Nineties the deconstruction was done on computer, alone.

With so many of these drum'n'bass or other electronica records being self-released and recorded by kids who didn't know how to play instruments in their rooms with computers and samplers, many saw fit to compare the genre to punk (I've even considered the Oval's *Systemisch* to be a digital-age counterpart to the first Ramones album, at least as a call to action and a crystalization of an underground movement). In fact it was more punk than punk, because it really did discard the hoary Sixties guitar rock tradition that the Pistols et al. claimed (disingenuously, as it turned out) to dismantle. Fair enough, although I would argue that punk and its offshoots' contribution to rock was not that you didn't have to know how to play an instrument to be in a band, but that you had to be interesting—musically and otherwise. The real punk bands formed as a collision of personalities (e.g., the Germs, the Sleepers, the Electric Eels); the ones that formed by stealing members from other bands (e.g., the Clash) or from auditions (the Sex Pistols) may as well have been the Eagles—or the Monkees. The difference between Half Japanese and Hall and

Oates is not that one band knows how to play their instruments and the other doesn't (don't ask which is which), or that one makes slick, high production records and the other makes raw, under-produced ones; the difference is that Hall and Oates are average people making average music, and Half Japanese are unusual people making unusual music. By the same token, when you lose the blend of interesting personalities, the music suffers—consider Pere Ubu in 1976 vs. Pere Ubu in 1996. I truly believe that Pete Townshend or Lou Reed have as much talent today as they did in the Sixties—but the lives they lead as established rock stars aren't as interesting as the lives they led as young writers and performers, which is why their music isn't as inspired or interesting.

But the big electronica takeover never quite happened; as Simon Reynolds has observed, it's the only musical movement that went from the underground straight to advertising without having any radio hits or producing any stars first. Just as folk labels like Elektra started releasing acid rock in the mid- to late-Sixties, labels that specialized in indie guitar rock like Matador and Caroline panicked and released or licensed a slew of electronica product, creating a synth dominated market that resembles, well, early Eighties new wave. I remember going to Rough Trade in London around 1996 or '97, and it was full of drum'n'bass 12-inches, with a bin about five inches wide for "indie rock." Around the same time I went to see Atari Teenage Riot at CBGB's. Especially given the venue, I felt sorry for all these kids going to see a high energy punk rock show minus the live band—the music was all sampled or pre-recorded. The band was committed but aurally it felt so cut-rate. It was the first time I ever felt old at CB's. I was 27 or 28 at the time. Still, we don't hear as much about "the death of guitar rock" now as we did a couple of years back. The year that everybody and their uncle did a drum'n'bass inspired album (Madonna, Clapton, Bowie) has had no more impact than the year everybody did a disco song (anyone got that Ethel Merman disco LP from '79?). Guitars sounded funny for a while (almost disrespectful) because people were still in mourning for Kurt Cobain, but eventually that wore off.

However, in the so-called illbient scene in New York, I did find the only truly New York music of the decade—it really sounded like New York did as I drifted through it in my early twenties, walking around for hours, enjoying being able to be there as an adult and not just a tourist kid. In this way, it was a kind of aural descendant of the Situationists concept of psychogeography, but it also sounded a hell of a lot like side three of *Electric Ladyland*. It wasn't noise music, it was about noises and synasthesia, and the collisions and near collisions that happen in the city every second of every day. Even Christian Marclay's earlier sound collages never really captured it that way. I went to Soundlab at David Linton's loft in Chinatown a few times. It was often hard to tell where the audience ended and the performance began—there was one DJ—but also pockets of other people doing sound as well. This also gives credence to the "new punk" charges. It was a cool scene before it started to fragment. Despite some media attention, it never really seemed to do anything commercially.

1995 was also when computers, and especially the Internet and e-mail, became a real presence in the indie music scene. Record sales went down, attributed to the fact that more people were surfing the Net than going to clubs or buying CDs. Many of the nascent internet pioneers (including my erstwhile bandmate and gURL.com co-founder Rebecca Odes) found it to be "the new punk rock" (and even Roger McGuinn compared it to the nascent folk/beatnik scene of the early Sixties). Many of the so-called "slackers" of the early Nineties who'd resisted stepping onto a career path were simply in a holding pattern until the Internet provided them a non-traditional (and thus acceptable) inroad to being a card carrying member of capitalist society. It turned that these people did care about money, they just weren't willing to sell their souls à la yuppies to do it—they just wanted to get paid for being creative, without becoming a cliché as either a yuppie or a bohemian. It started off as a grass roots movement, but it didn't take long before it went corporate. After all, unlike starting a hippie commune or wearing a mohawk, nobody ever started a Web site to drop out of society—it was another way of engaging society. But I'm not really condemning the people who were there before anyone figured out how to make money off of it, I'm talking about the latecomers who cashed in without doing time in Reagan/Bush recessionville. It took baby boomers well over a decade to sell out, it took the Internet generation less than half of one.

Actually, MTV provides an interesting precedent for the Net. Originally run by folks in their early twenties with an "anything goes" attitude and met with skepticism by older businessmen, within a couple of years it had become so huge that it sold out to Viacom and stopped taking chances. The Internet boom is also a little like the acid revolution of the mid-Sixties. John Coltrane claimed that on acid he "perceived the interrelationship of all living things"; on the Internet you're connected to every living thing that has a modem, that virtual third eye. Acid produced a "trip" which induced spiritual awakenings; the Internet is an "information superhighway" that has no religious overtones—it's mostly a big mall. Of course, there's no bad trips or lacings with speed or who knows what else either—a safer drug for safer times. Then again, acid brought you Beefheart's *Trout Mask Replica*, Skip Spence's *Oar*, Syd Barrett, Ken Kesey, *Zap* comix, and some of Philip K. Dick's and Kenneth Anger's finest work; the Internet brought you...the pets.com sock puppet? In the Sixties, the President was shot, the country went to war for ten years in Asia, Charles Manson had his followers carve up a celebrity's wife out in L.A., and the Beatles were elected to two terms in office. In the Nineties, the John Lennon figure shot himself after three albums, the stud in the White House hung in there for eight years (character assassination doesn't count), the war (in the mid-East this time) only took a month, a celebrity took matters into his own hands and practically beheaded his own wife in L.A., and the kids dropped out first, then later tuned in and turned on (their Macs) right around the same time Jennifer Aniston ditched the gourmet coffee waitressing gig on *Friends*. A far more sensible scenario, no? Like Bill Murray finally winning Andie MacDowell's heart after living the same day over and over in the movie *Groundhog Day*, the U.S. of A. finally got it right after two decades of retakes. No wonder the economy got so good! It's like the whole decade was an Oliver Stone script rewrite of the Sixites, complete with historical remixing and a happy ending.

> *How could one ever think anything's permanent?*
> "Stablemate," Will Oldham, 1996

And then there's the impermanence of digital technology. Computers deal in virtual reality. Unless you print something out, you generally have nothing to show for hours spent on a computer once you shut it off. There's an overload of data available on the internet, yet it cannot be archived—100 years from now no one will know what happened in the first five years of the Internet. We know what happened in the first five years of cinema, of photography, of recorded music. Is that progress? This acceptance of a lack of permanence, is, I think, partly responsible for the younger generation's increased awareness of and enthusiasm for improvisation. Something that exists in the moment, and then is gone—that's something the digital world is all about. Web sites last for how long—a couple of years? In the art world we see more video art installations, less painting and sculpture. CDs are not archival. They may not go blank in twenty years, as some originally thought, but they won't last forever.

Not only that, but for me and for many other people I know, they don't lend themselves to repeated listening. Since everything is right up front aurally on a CD, you hear it all the first time you listen. It takes a few spins of vinyl to hear everything through the murk, and then sometimes only on headphones. It's like the difference between candlelight and a fluorescent light bulb. Besides insisting on revealing every aural secret (and often including every outtake as "bonus tracks"), CDs also never let you forget your precise temporal location in the recording from second to second by providing a digital time readout on the CD player. They're almost designed to eliminate the mystery both from the original recording and the experience of listening. Also the imaging—literally, where you visualize the sounds when you face your speakers—is way off with CDs. Sounds seems to coming from all sorts of weird angles and corners of the room. It's just not natural sound replication. Everything about CDs is disposable—they're small, you just listen to them once, and they won't last. If alternative rock was just another part of the alternative-minded America of the early Nineties, then CDs have become simply part of the digital world of the new millennium—after all, you can even play them on your computer. Eliminating the mystery also eliminates people's curiosity, and when that happens people become less intelligent. In that way CDs are part of the "dumbing down" phenomena that many commented on in the early Nineties.

The beginning of the end, though, was the introduction of stereo. Contrary to popular wisdom, mono is much truer and more powerful sound replication than stereo. Just check out any Stones, Beatles, or Dylan record from the Sixties in mono—the sound is thicker and more focused. Even the album jackets boasted slightly larger images than the reproductions on their stereo counterparts, hinting that stereo version is a reduction of the mono original (of course CD reissues miniaturize the album cover image even further). Multi-tracking diffuses the sound, separating it into little subdivisions that you have to put back together again in the mix, then repositioning them, by panning, like layering cells in animation, is crazy. When you listen to a mono mix there's a depth of field, like there is when you watch a movie. That's lost in a stereo mix. In fact, I'd even suggest that rock's slide into corporate culture began with the introduction of stereo. The music is ill-suited for stereo, and even worse for digital sound. Rock was forced to comply with an industry standard that cut its sonic power in half (literally). I only recently learned that most club P.A. systems are in mono. This illuminates at least part of my preference for live music as opposed to records, and accentuates the directness of the live experience.

And consider this: virtually every major counterculture group in the Sixties had a song with "together" in the title. "We Can Be Together" (Jefferson Airplane), "We Could Be So Good Together" (the Doors), "Come Together" (Beatles, MC5), "All Together Now" (Beatles), "Join Together" (the Who), even those notorious peace'n'love-buzzkills the Velvet Underground had "We're Gonna Have a Real Good Time Together." There were Human Be-In's and communes...togetherness was a defining and powerful characteristic of the times. Stereo separation, best appreciated in solitude on headphones, was symbolic of The Man's efforts to disperse the "hippie" movement and helped usher in the Me Decade.

From a November 1998 interview I did with Canadian artist/filmmaker/musician Michael Snow:

> Michael Snow: I don't know, I think life is pretty interesting, but to tell you the truth, I think it's been downhill for the human race since the invention of agriculture.
>
> Alan Licht: Why is that?
>
> Michael Snow: Well, in hunting and gathering societies, there wasn't a way of making a living, what you were doing was living. And you had to recognize what everything out there was, and what use it was or wasn't to you, and if it was dangerous. So there was less compartmentalizing than there is now, and it was possible to feel in terms of temperature and sensory possibilities. Obviously it was difficult—people starved, etc. But as a general ridiculous argument, it was probably a more integrated way of living. There was no separation between looking for something to eat and being alive.

Life was cooler when it was live to two-track—now it's just *overproduced*. If we can agree that something like an Alan Parsons Project LP is the lowest form of rock and roll, then post-primitive human existence is the lowest form of life. For human beings to walk around thinking they're superior to other animals is ludicrous—if anything, we're inferior. Sure, a gopher can't write a symphony or an

Ellingtonian jazz suite, but it can't write an Air Supply song either. I've never seen a raccoon stage an inquisition, hold a slave auction, or build a concentration camp—have you? Our "superior" "intelligence" is a massive biological mistake. "Standing in line we're aberrations/Defects in a defect's mirror...Progressed to a point of no distinction/Dementia of a higher order," Darby Crash spews forth on the Germs' "What We Do Is Secret." He's not talking about the people in the band, or the L.A. punk scene, or "freaks" everywhere— he means the whole race, babe (in "Manimal" he "sings," "If I'm just an animal/Then I can do no wrong/But they say I'm something better/So I gotta hold on").

Begins with a blessing/and it ends with a curse/
Making life easy/by making it worse
"Why Are We Sleeping?" Soft Machine, 1968

Computers also continue the trend away from communalism towards personal isolation. Okay, obviously you're connected to more people, potentially, than ever before thanks to the Internet. And equally obviously, you're just sitting alone looking into your monitor while you do it. People used to gather in the church or the town square; then it was the movie theatre or concert hall, or wherever. Now that home entertainment threatens to be completely downloadable through a computer, and that literally any kind of shopping can be done on a computer, will there be any reason to go out? Of course there will, but consider this analogy: At one time there was just one town movie theatre, which had to cater to a lot of different tastes. At one time commerical TV and radio was the same way. Years ago I saw Martin Scorsese introduce a screening of Jacques Tati's *Playtime* at the Museum of Modern Art, and he marvelled that when he was a kid a Tati film was shown on local television and the next day all the kids at school were talking about it. Can you imagine a foreign film shown on TV in prime time now? Geoffrey O'Brien has written of the Sixties that "the Top 40 sound of any given moment was likely to be a curious amalgam of disparate elements, 'Strangers in the Night' followed immediately by 'Papa's Got A Brand New Bag,' the Troggs in regular rotation with Herb Alpert and the Tijuana Brass. A hit was a hit." When the large companies realize that higher quality product will be produced independently (hello DIY labels and John Cassavetes), they start just producing the mediocre shit that will appeal to the masses, which then tends to fragment and compartmentalize as the people with actual taste will have to abandon the major outlets and find or create those that cater to their needs. The movie theatre is replaced by a multiplex and maybe an arthouse, but also by videos and DVDs. Network TV is supplemented if not outright replaced by cable TV and now TiVo, which allows the ultimate in home programming and recording—you even select your own commercials. AM radio is replaced by commercial FM radio, college radio, and now MP3s. FM radio started off doing free-form, off-the-wall stuff; then it became formularized. College radio sometimes attempts to pick up the slack, but just as often winds up following the trends out of a lack of imagination or sheer laziness. The critic and composer Tom Johnson has likened the experimental music scene to Off-Off-Broadway, "which began around ten years ago [he's writing in 1977] as vital experimental genre with brilliant discoveries every season, and then gradually became a sort of farm-club for commercial theatre." He could just as well be talking about non–Top-40 radio programming.

But maybe it's just me. It all comes back to the idea that I generally don't depend on broadcast media for entertainment, but I wish

I could. I've always been a big fan of watching movies on TV; I don't care about commercials or editing. Especially growing up, it was a way of finding out about the world without leaving the house, and seeing something like *Taxi Driver* on TV, injected into in my safe suburban New Jersey living room as a teenager, was really an eye-opening experience. When I was a kid, they showed *The Wizard of Oz* every year, and everybody talked about it on the school bus the next day. As a teenager, *The Day After*, which showed the aftermath of a nuclear holocaust, aired and everybody watched it and talked about it at school the next day. Nobody does that with the Internet—it's too fragmented. Each of these other mediums started off with a limited selection—that was the unifying principle. The only reason MTV played all those new wave videos to begin with was because their library was so limited they had to play whatever they could in order to broadcast 24 hours a day. The Web's so-called "information explosion" has always meant a virtually unlimited selection—which discourages any sense of real community.

I wonder if this has something to do with the fact that there's, like, no competition now in the rock scene—everyone just seems to do their own thing. The cool thing about the Sixties was the Beatles, Stones, Dylan, Beach Boys, etc., trying to top each other with each successive album, or ripping off each other's styles or songs. What made bands like the Byrds or Buffalo Springfield so great was they were talented folkies who wanted to be bigger than the Beatles. Even through most of the Nineties bands seemed to at least be trying to give either Nirvana or Dinosaur or Sonic Youth or My Bloody Valentine or Pavement a run for their money by copping their shit and trying to one up them. Who is Belle and Sebastian trying to be better than? Or Elliott Smith? Or Sleater Kinney? Aztec Camera? The Zombies? George Harrison? The Clash? Or nobody at all? I like all those bands, but that's no way to have an exciting scene, a scene that matters, without that competition. Part of the glory of rock stardom, like the glory of a champion athelete or a gunslinger, is knowing that there's some young punk who wants to be just like you, only better. I don't see that out there right now.

But I don't want to get too down on computers. Word processing beats typewriters, e-mail blows away both the phone and regular mail for communication, and when we reach the stage where owning a computer is like having a good university library in your own home (access to all kinds of books and periodicals from the past century or so), it will be an incredible tool—and is already. But in the same way that candlelight is nicer than a fluorescent lightbulb, if not as practical, I still prefer vinyl to CD, or finding an out of print book in a used book shop unexpectedly to the short cuts afforded by computers and the Internet.

III.
ON THE MORNING AFTER THE NINETIES

I recently wrote to a friend saying that rock was now in a mid-life crisis; in the Fifties it was in its infancy, in the Sixties it was developing its personality like a ten-year-old, the punk thing was like teenage rebellion, grunge and all that was like your late twenties and early thirties, when you've got some experience but are still young enough to be energetic and engaged. Seeing the current crop of chest-beating, macho fratboy rockers like Limp Bizkit, Blink 182, or Korn is not particularly encouraging; wasn't it jock assholes like these that were beating Kurt Cobain up every day at school? I could see part of my skinny-ass self in Mick Jones or Iggy or Mick Jagger or Prince when I was a kid; I can't see myself anywhere in the musclebound posturings of Limp Bizkit's Fred Durst and his ilk. If Woodstock '94 was a grunge update of the original, Woodstock '99 was practically Altamont in contrast, with multiple rapes, fires, and general chaos— but at least at Altamont Mick Jagger feebly implored the crowd to "cool out"; Fred Durst told the Woodstock '99 mob, "I don't think you should mellow out."

The current domination of these shirtless rap-metal thugs on the one hand and the Britney Spearses and 'N Syncs on the other may not bode well, but neither did the just pre-Beatles Bobby-riddled horizon of forty years ago (Rydell, Darin, et al). This too shall pass. I think it was John Cassavetes that said that love is like a watch, where it stops and then you have to wind it up for it to start ticking again, and I think that applies to rock as well—or at least my enthusiasm for it.

In the meantime, I'm happy to say that the Eighties' indie vets I've seen perform recently have all been tremendous. I opened for

Fugazi at Maxwell's in the summer of '98 and they sounded better than ever. All the years of touring have given them the kind of telepathy other bands can only dream of. I'd never seen Steve Albini play before All Tomorrow's Parties 2000, but Shellac was the highlight of the festival—Steve still rocks the ultimate antagonistic guitar sound, the rhythm section is formidable, and Bob Weston is pretty quick with the comebacks during the Q and A sessions. Calvin Johnson did a solo acoustic thing at this year's NY Underground Film Festival and his singing was great—he sounded just like Johnny Cash. On the "Enough With the Piss Bag" fall 2000 tour, Mike Watt and the Pair of Pliers put on my favorite show of the year—sharp playing, lotsa great covers, totally high energy (even from Watt, who's still recovering from grave illness). As the crowd was cheering at the end, Watt said, "It means a lot to me that I can still take the Boat [his van] out on tour." Now that the alterna-dust has settled, it's good to see people who were way ahead of the trend still thriving and still in touch with what made them good—or what made them want to be good—in the first place. The real punk rock dream was not that the world would be a better place if punk was popular; it was for your heroes to not suck ten to fifteen years down the line, like the Sixties rock aristocracy did. As far as I'm concerned, these guys have fulfilled that dream.

From *No Logo: Taking Aim at the Brand Bullies* by Naomi Klein (Picador USA, 2000)

"When the youth-culture feeding frenzy began in the early nineties, many of us who were young at the time saw ourselves as victims of a predatory marketing machine that co-opted our identities, our styles, and our ideas and turned them into brand food. Nothing was immune; not punk, not hip-hop, not fetish, not techno...Few of us asked, at least not right away, why it was that these scenes and ideas were proving so packageable, so unthreatening—and so profitable. Many of us had been certain were doing something subversive and rebellious but....what was it again? In retrospect, a central problem was the mostly unquestioned assumption that just because a scene or a style is different (that is, new and not yet mainstream), it necessarily exists in opposition to the mainstream, rather simply sitting unthreateningly in its margins. Many of us assumed that "alternative"—music that was hard to listen to, styles that were hard to look at—was also anti-commerical..."

From "Fauxhemian Rhapsody" by Rob Walker, *New York Times Magazine*, January 23, 2000:

"Being bohemian — or counterculture, or alternative or whatever you want to call it — used to be all about dichotomy: you chose one life at the expense of another. Opt out of corporate life to run a literary magazine, and you had to live in a fifth-floor walkup, shop in thrift stores, drive an old VW bug and eat at hole-in-the-wall cafes. On the other hand, you got to cling to your unsullied ideals and aesthetic sense. For many, the bohemian life was just a youthful phase. You could have your freedom for so long, then you had to go work for the Man. Now, of course, it's difficult to find an actual bohemian, yet boho trappings that vaguely suggest counterculture taste are everywhere, because the fauxhemian idea is that you don't have to choose anymore. You can be mainstream and alternative, a grown-up and a hipster, all at the same time.

Conspicuous consumption no longer cancels out the idealistic self-image....Miramax, an "indie" film company whose marketing department sprays an intellectual mist onto its usually middlebrow product, is a fauxhemian juggernaut. Janeane Garofalo, who stars opposite Uma Thurman or Sylvester Stallone part of the time and rolls her eyes about mainstream Hollywood the rest of the time, is our fauxhemian It Girl. And Apple Computer's C.E.O., Steve Jobs, a centimillionaire in bluejeans and a black mock turtleneck, embodies the look and feel of fauxhemian chic.

La vie fauxhéme is a peculiar artifact of the bust-to-boom 1990s. The decade started on a slackerish note, as a generation of Americans was informed it would probably be the first not to match its parents' income. Since the Man was laying everybody off, why not grow a goatee, chase those dreams and forget about growing up and making money? Of course, the intervening years played out differently. Real money has found its way to younger and younger people, crashing directly into the postundergrad second-hand-shop lifestyle.

What's more, a lot of that money has gone to people who never bothered to pay their dues by groveling before Eighties-style Master of the Universe bosses. The cultural equivalent of dropping out to write poetry became dropping out to write Linux code—the open-source, anticapitalist computer-operating system—though plenty of people are making real money even off that.

A result is that corporate America has not only stopped trying to homogenize its new recruits, it is also practically begging college dropouts with nose rings to explain what the hell is going on out there. And gradually that old dichotomy has fallen away. What if you could just, you know, telecommute for the Man? Or maybe do a little consulting gig, only this one time? Or let's say the Man wants to put a million dollars of seed capital behind some side project you've been working on in your dorm—or help your nascent literary Webzine go public.

Still, as this generation unlearned its expectations of failure, it never unlearned its love of bohemianism; it just reconfigured bohemianism to accommodate a grown-up income. It's one of the few traits it shares with its parents' generation: a widespread reluctance to grow up all the way. Whatever his or her age, the fauxhemian is not one of those stick-in-the-mud, conventional, middle-class grown-ups.

So it's critical at least to pretend to keep any middle-class definition of success at arm's length: it's O.K. to like the theory of a Parisian bistro or the practice of a boutique eatery like Pastis; eating at a strip-mall chain called Pastis Too!, however, would be unacceptable."

This is the legacy of "Smells Like Teen Spirit" and the President who's a Coltrane fan—"You can be mainstream and alternative, all at the same time." Urban Bohemia is the new suburbia; neither here nor there. Like where I grew up, which had Macy's and Bloomingdale's just like the Big Apple, but fresh air and houses and backyards. Like Eighties new wave, too watered down to be punk, but too offbeat to be standard-issue major-label rock. Like smoking pot but not inhaling. It's a very comfortable existence, but culturally it's stilted. We've remade suburbia in our own image. Nobody wants to be like the Sixties cliché of wearing bell-bottoms and long hair in your teens and going corporate in your thirties, and no one really asked for punk rock to become popular—it just was, all of a sudden. Everything Gen X got interested in got co-opted whether it was punk rock, independent cinema, or the Internet. We dealt with it the best we could, generally without falling into some of the traps that previous generations have.

The popularity of Ralph Nader's candidacy during the 2000 campaign is the legacy of social semi-responsibility. Nader played Pastis to Gore's Pastis Too! Naively thinking that Bush's stupidity would result in a shoo-in Gore victory (didn't anybody remember Reagan? Or *Forrest Gump*?), aging Xers' political consciousness was awakened by an "alternative" candidate the same way their ambition had been sparked by an "alternative" career path with the Internet. As if they were choosing Sleater-Kinney over Britney Spears and Christina Aguilera; as if they were choosing an outsider like Daniel Johnston over a couple of president's/senator's sons like Jakob Dylan or Sean Lennon; as if the next logical step from a rock and roll president was a punk rock president; as if they had the luxury of assuaging their fauxhemian guilt over creating the new economy by committing to an anti-corporate left wing candidate with no commercial potential (I'm surprised no one made a CORPORATE CANDIDATES STILL SUCK T-shirt). I'll bet playing his guitar at a Nader rally or two sure made Eddie Vedder feel less like a corporate rocker. A Nader vote was like a magic wand to make you punk rock again. It was my generation's Deadhead sticker on a Cadillac.

Norman Mailer has recently commented that because America is such a puritanical country, Americans become anxious if they have too much money. This election was all about relieving that anxiety. The last economic expansion that lasted as long as the Clinton one was from 1960 to 1968—ending when Nixon (a proven loser) was elected. There were two candidates in 2000 that no one could be confident in—George W. Bush, with his outright stupidity and ignorance, and Nader, with his total lack of governing experience and dilapidated physiognomy. By electing either of these two men, consumer confidence would disappear and the economy would go down the tubes—and so would the puritanical anxiety. While supporting the Green Party when Nader played spoiler in the face of a Bush victory may have seemed like rearranging the furniture while the house burns down (to borrow a metaphor from Naomi Klein about identity politics), psychologically it made all the sense in the world.

Many have accused the Florida government and the Supreme Court of partisanship or corruption in the handling of the 2000 election. Yet in truth they astutely gauged the group fantasy of the Mayflower masses and acted accordingly. If Gore, the winner of the popular, and most likely, electoral votes, had been allowed into office, it would mean four more years of boom economy. The puritanical national psyche demanded that he not be allowed to govern, and bum rushed the incompetent Dubya into office. Now Bush Jr. is filling the White House with some of daddy's favorite advisors, getting into Star Wars, promoting tax cuts for the rich in order to prevent the inevitable recession which he was forced into office to *create*, and singing the rest of the Reagan/Bush hit parade—*you can forget about a song but never really forget it.*

If the next decade turns into a rerun of the Eighties—if there haven't been any lasting changes from the early Nineties embrace of reality, when "everybody" was "hip," if the Reagan/Bush empire never ended (to paraphrase Philip K. Dick, who believed that the delivery girl's jewel alerted him to the current, parallel existence of the ancient Roman Empire, which in fact had never ended)—then we've blown it. I suspect we may have come up short of real greatness, but it always was (and is) a generation of under-achievers. After all, I'm calling this sucker a book, and it's only 76 pages long.